Williamson, Mitch
Safe Riding

DATE DUE

SAFE RIDING
Staying Alive on Your Motorcycle

Keep the Shiny Side Up!

Mitch Williamson

Oct. 17, 1993

Safe Riding

Staying Alive on Your Motorcycle

THE COMPLETE SAFETY MANUAL

Mitch Williamson

*Introduction by Charles F. Livingston,
Associate Administrator,
National Highway Traffic Safety Administration*

EVEREST HOUSE  PUBLISHERS

New York

Library of Congress Cataloging in Publication Data:
Williamson, Mitch.
   Safe riding.
       New York   Everest House
   Bibliography, p. 211
   Includes index.
   1. Motorcycling—Safety measures.   I. Title.
   GV1060.4.W54   1980   796.7'5   80-11435
   ISBN: 0-89696-098-6

The author wishes to thank the Motorcycle Industry
Council, Inc. for permission to reprint the State Motorcyle Equipment Requirements chart, and the Motorcycle Safety Foundation for permission to reprint the State
Motorcycle Operator Licensing Procedures chart.

ACKNOWLEDGEMENTS

In addition to the reference sources listed at the back of the book, I would like to give special thanks to one invaluable research source. At the Oklahoma State Department of Public Safety, I was given free access to the fatality files involving motorcycle operators, and a desk at which to work in the Safety Records Division under the direction of Mr. George Moore. State Trooper Don Wyckoff, in charge of the motorcycle training for beginning riders, was especially helpful both in personal interviews and in supplying useful source materials.

CONTENTS

*Metal surfaces. Broken paving. Grease and oil slicks.
Litter and debris. Dips and bumps. Bridges and guard
rails. Pets and people.*

PREFACE

Staying alive on two wheels in street or highway traffic is a genuine, triple-plated achievement for *any* cyclist. This is true regardless of his or her age, or the amount of money paid for the bike. I came to this conclusion quickly after becoming a "commuter" cyclist; and many thousands of miles later, I'm more convinced of it than ever.

Statistics bear me out. With motorcycle registrations since 1961 rising about eight times as fast as the increase in all motor vehicles, the motorcycle death rate based on mileage is five to six times higher than it is for other motor vehicles.[1, 3] In 1978, about three fatalities to motorcycle operators occurred nationwide for every 100 accidents involving the two-wheelers.[2] In the brief span from 1975 to 1978, when motorcycle registrations increased only 3.5% in the United States (to 5,138,000), motorcycle fatalities rose by a gruesome 41.1%![3] One report indicates that the cycle rider "has a greater probability of being killed in an accident than the user of any other conventional means of transportation."[4]

This is hard to take, but easy to understand—on a motorcycle, you're exposed and vulnerable. No wraparound frame of welded steel; no crash bumpers. Just you and the thundering herd on every side, everyone seemingly hell-bent-for-election to get somewhere before you do. You're competing with motorists who know they can come through dozens of fender-benders with no more worry than the size of their deductible . . . and they'll certainly come out ahead in

[1] National Safety Council. "Motorcycle Facts" (*Sept. 1978*)

[2] Motorcycle Safety Foundation. "Motorcycle Statistics" (*1978*)

[3] National Highway Traffic Safety Administration. "Motorcycle Accident Data Summary" (*1979*)

[4] "Motorcycle Accident Research"—Study sponsored by the Motorcycle Safety Foundation and presented by Martin L. Reiss, BioTechnology, Inc. at the Foundation's Motorcycle Operator Testing Workshop (*Oct. 1974*)

any encounter with a biker. You, on the other hand, face such sobering statistics as this one published in the May 1976 American Journal of Public Health:

> "For the nation as a whole, close to 90 per cent of all motorcycle crashes result in injury or death, compared to 10 per cent of automobile crashes."

In Oklahoma during 1978, there was an accident resulting in death or injury to the cyclist for every 70 motorcycle registrations in the state.[5]

Annual Motorcycle Rider Deaths

YEAR	FATALITIES	YEAR	FATALITIES	YEAR	FATALITIES
1960	731	1966	2,043	1972	2,700
1961	697	1967	1,971	1973	3,130
1962	759	1968	1,900	1974	3,160
1963	882	1969	1,960	1975	2,800
1964	1,118	1970	2,330	1976	3,000
1965	1,515	1971	2,410	1977	3,870*

*The 1977 figure averaged more than 10 deaths per day!

Your most likely time for an accident comes during the first six months of ownership. The most accident-prone group of cycle riders is the youngest: those under 20. The value of experience is proved by the fact that in this same high-rate age group, riders with less than six months' experience have twice as many motorcycle accidents as others. One study showed 20% of inexperienced cyclists have their first accident on their first or second ride![6]

For one thing, there is no safe and easy way to learn how to ride a motorcycle—just ways that are safer and easier than others. These are covered early in this book. You probably won't find anyone officially teaching first-timers how to ride unless you live in a good-sized

[5] Oklahoma Department of Public Safety. "Motorcycle Accident Facts" (1978)

[6] National Safety Council. "Safety Education Data Sheet No. 98," Revised

or progressive community; and even then, what they can do is limited. They can't sit at your side, as a driver training instructor does in an automobile, ready to take over when you panic or simply pull a dumb trick.

Another hard fact: every driver on the streets with four wheels has to be considered an opponent in traffic, whether it's because he doesn't see you (and many motorists don't, unbelievable as it may seem), or because he is antagonistic toward you and all cycle riders, as many motorists are.

Don't get me wrong. In spite of all this, a good motorcycle is, in my opinion, the way to go when you have no need to carry passengers or cargo too big or heavy for a bike. It's transportation that puts you "out in the open" where the air feels good (my wife mistakenly thinks all I do is inhale exhaust fumes). It's energy-conserving and costs a comparative pittance for gas. It gives you a sense of accomplishment not possible with four wheels and nothing to do but tap an accelerator, and brake and steer with power. And it develops your sense of balance, peripheral vision and full-body alertness in a way that will keep you younger and more fit than your car-driving neighbor.

You can only know what I mean by experiencing it; I recommend it wholeheartedly *unless* (1) you think it would be a good way to show how brave you are; (2) you want to take it up to impress the opposite sex; or (3) you think it would be nice to get places faster by being able to dart in and out of traffic where even the compacts can't go.

But the fact remains, too many riders are getting killed or injured because new cyclists are too much on their own with no practical safety tips drilled into them. Driver's manuals tell us that "at least 9 out of 10 accidents are caused by human error." If this is the case, we can choose to be safe or unsafe in our driving; and if you choose safety on your motorcycle, this book will give you the straight facts you need to ride safely.

If I had read a book like this before I took that first ride to work on my shiny new Honda, I would *not* have gone into the curb, damaging both of us on the way home. A few months later I would *not* have gone down on the street in a split second with the risk of becoming a crushed human torch. A year later I would *not* have banged up my headlight and handlebars, rear-ending the car ahead during a left turn . . . and on and on.

There are quite a few books on the subject of cycling; but here are some features unique to this one:

- All of the safety tips given here are the result of hard experience—my own, plus that of motorcycle safety instructors, motorcycle police, cyclists with exceptional mileage backgrounds (both street and highway riders), and cycle dealers and service people.

- I know of no other work as complete as this book in the number of hazard situations covered, and what to do to avoid accidents, written in specific, easy-to-understand language.

- All of the safety tips in this book are accompanied by actual case histories of cyclist fatalities involving the exact hazard discussed. You are told precisely what happened, why it happened, and what the cyclist could have done to prevent the accident—even when a motorist caused it.

- The contents are highly specialized. Nothing on dirt-bike fun or racing . . . nothing about repairing or customizing cycles. Just hundreds of pages of tried-and-proven ways of staying alive in traffic on your motorcycle.

- This book is thoroughly practical. It can save your life, if you'll let it. Study it until the advice it contains becomes a part of your subconscious reflexes. The stakes are worth the effort.

Yours for safe riding . . . "keep the shiny side up and the black side down!"

MITCH WILLIAMSON

Oklahoma City
August 1980

INTRODUCTION

The advice in this book will substantially increase your chances of avoiding an accident and the serious injury which often results from motorcycle crashes if you consider carefully *in advance* the dangers that are always present in motorcycle riding.

Motorcycling can be fun and exciting, but it also has inherent risks. Very few motorcyclists have not crashed at one time or another—the lucky ones lived to tell about it. The unlucky ones became statistics which cast a gruesome shadow over motorcycling as a sport and means of transportation. Mitch Williamson discusses both types of crashes in this book to give the novice rider a guide to survival on a motorcycle. It contains much practical experience of many skilled and experienced riders. Blended with the accumulated wisdom of the survivors are tragic examples of why this advice is so important.

No one likes to read about the senseless destruction of our fellow human beings. The accident case histories aren't pretty. However, they are important because they are graphic evidence of what can happen if a motorcyclist fails to use practical motorcycling safety measures. Therefore, those fatalities will not be totally in vain if they convince new motorcyclists to avoid the errors which caused the accidents.

Motorcycles are a major form of transportation in this country. They will grow even more important as fuel prices rise higher and higher and fuel shortages become more frequent. If each motorcyclist rides safely, motorcycling can be a relatively economic, efficient and enjoyable form of transportation. If not, motorcycling will continue to be the most hazardous form of motor transportation a person can choose.

Charles F. Livingston
Associate Administrator
National Highway Traffic Safety
Administration

SAFE RIDING
Staying Alive on Your Motorcycle

1. What is a Safe Age to Begin?

D0 YOU KNOW that as of this writing, 15 of our 50 states will legally license children under 16 to operate motorcycles on their streets and highways? Eight states will issue licenses at 14; seven others at age 15. After lengthy research of motorcycle accident fatality records, I am convinced beyond doubt that these ages are too young to ride a motorcycle in traffic.

Think about it: one or two years *before* these states will permit boys and girls to drive an automobile (providing far more protection), they legally turn them loose on a motorcycle! In these age brackets, our young people are 15 to 20 times as likely to be killed in a motorcycle accident as they would be if operating an automobile! On the face of it, this has to be the most ridiculous inconsistency of today's lawmakers. Legal or not, my strong advice is: *wait until you are 16 before riding a motorcycle!*

Some Sobering Case Histories

Before you conclude I am a prejudiced "square," look at these case histories.

In one fatal accident, a licensed 14-year-old was riding as a passenger while his 12-year-old brother operated his 100 cc cycle at only 25–30 miles per hour on a country road. The vehicle that ran into the boys was only going 10–15 miles per hour when its driver failed to yield properly at an intersection. Even so, the impact carried the boys up and over the car into a ditch, killing them both. The 14-year-old was not legally permitted to carry passengers; but at age 14 you may be prone to make exceptions. A cycle of that size isn't even engineered for two passengers; but few 14-year-olds worry about such things when a younger brother pleads for a chance at the throttle. At this age, you also may depend too much on "having the right-of-way." Youthfulness had to be a contributing factor in this tragedy.

You may be telling yourself the size of the cycle might have been the problem. It is true that the smaller, less powerful bikes to which younger riders are limited are harder to see and have too little power for evasive action in emergencies. But take the case of a 13-year-old operating a 360 cc on the streets of a large city with a 14-year-old passenger holding on. Heading into a curving downgrade, the operator hit 60 miles per hour in a 40-miles-per-hour zone and pulled left of the centerline for a head-on collision with a pickup truck. Both boys were ejected from the motorcycle and were dead on arrival. This operator, of course, was unlicensed. Would the result have been different with the 14-year-old up front? These are ages when the temptation to speed is great; and lack of experience coupled with excessive speed is a deadly combination. More horses in this case may even have encouraged the speeding. So, size of cycle won't compensate for immature judgment.

Other motorcycle fatalities in my state during recent years include the following situations, briefly stated:

- A 14-year-old speeding on a wet dirt road at night, on a 250 cc. Thrown from cycle by deep rut.

- Two 14-year-olds, one on a 125 cc, the other on a 100 cc. Both wiped out by a 16-year-old speeder when one cyclist started a U-turn.

- A 15-year-old operating a 125 cc at night with no lights, no helmet, no license, no meaningful experience; carrying another 15-year-old as passenger. Collided left of county road centerline with his own 13-year-old brother on another 125 cc. One dead, two badly injured.

- 14-year-old operating 100 cc at night without helmet, and with 13-year-old sister as passenger. At 10 miles per hour over the speed limit, topped a rise and hit a cow in the road. Boy killed, girl injured.

- An 8-year-old operating a 75 cc with his 6-year-old sister as passenger, struck by a speeding pickup driven by unlicensed 15-year-old. Boy killed, girl injured.

- A 14-year-old on a 200 cc, killed when a tractor turned left in front of him with the boy overtaking at 50 miles per hour.

- A 13-year-old operating a 100 cc, with a 15-year-old passenger. Turned left without signaling, struck by semitrailer tractor. Both boys killed.

- A 14-year-old on a 125 cc following close behind a truck, made a sharp left turn and collided with fast-moving pickup. Killed instantly.

- A 15-year-old on a 100 cc, carrying a 15-year-old passenger, tried unsuccessfully to beat a freight train at a crossing. Both killed.

At a glance, you have seen that some of these young riders were killed as a direct result of their own recklessness and negligence; others because of improper actions by motorists. Some of these case histories will be dealt with in other chapters discussing specific hazards. My whole point in this brief listing is simply to stress one fact: Under 16, children are too young to deal with traffic emergencies of any kind, let alone on motorcycles with their inherent lack of protection!

The National Safety Council says most state studies "show from 42 to 66 per cent of the motorcyclists in accidents are under 20 years of age."

In March 1978 the Motorcycle Safety Foundation published an analysis of 51,480 motorcycle accident reports for a single year. One finding stands out: "Most motorcycle accidents (40%) occur to motorcyclists under 20 years of age."

One more good reason to wait until you are 16 is cited in a publication of the American Driver and Traffic Safety Education Association. Most motorcycle accidents involve an automobile or other motor vehicle, so it helps a beginning cyclist to know something about operating a car as well. As the Association puts it, "driver education establishes the basic traffic safety education concepts. An understanding of car operator capabilities and other vehicle limitations and performance ranges will result in improved coexistence on the highways. Most current motorcycle instructional materials, media and other resources are designed with the assumption that automobile education has been completed. The materials rely on the student's possessing driver education information in order to perform in a specialized motorcycle course."

Before leaving this subject, here is one more case history. A 14-year-old was operating a 100 cc cycle, with a 15-year-old passenger. The operator had been drinking; and perhaps because of this, he went into a curve left of the centerline at 35 miles per hour. A pickup going the same speed laid down 43 feet of skid marks before the impact, and 26 feet after the head-on collision. The cycle passenger was thrown off and suffered injuries; the 14-year-old died under the cycle. This boy was handicapped by an illegal passenger on a cycle not built for two, and by operating his bike under the influence of alcohol. He went into the curve at the maximum legal speed for his cycle (too fast under the conditions), and he left his proper driving lane. Now, these judgment and operational errors *could* happen at any age. At 14, they are *more apt* to happen. Don't try to operate a motorcycle before you are 16 years old—and when you do, get the best training you can find!

2. Learning to Ride and Getting Experience

IF YOU ARE an experienced motorist, you may drive greatly relaxed—perhaps with only one hand on the power steering wheel, and enjoying music and air conditioning. You ride in the strong, steel-enclosed framework of a vehicle providing road-hugging weight and four-wheel stability. But on a cycle, that protection and stability are gone, and you ride exposed to traffic and the elements. Your body must be more alert, because it is more active. Your hands, for example, not only assist in steering, but also operate your clutch, throttle, front brake, turn signals, horn and light switches. It's an entirely different operation, and you must be trained and become experienced in these differences if you want to ride with comparative safety.

A survey of hospital patients in Minnesota showed that 20% of those admitted following motorcycle accidents were riding for their first or second time. Fully 70% had rented or borrowed the cycle. According to one North Carolina Highway Safety Research Center study (based on operating miles), borrowers of motorcycles were involved in nearly 12 times as many accidents as cycle owners. When you borrow a motorcycle, it's usually for the purpose of "trying it out" to see whether you'd like one for yourself. That means you most likely have had neither the training nor the experience necessary to insure safety.

A major contributing factor cited in a study of North Carolina University students injured or killed in motorcycle accidents was "lack of knowledge of operation of the vehicle." The three most-needed areas of knowledge, according to the report, were turning skill (see Chapter 21), stopping (Chapter 19), and riding properly in traffic (and that's what this entire book is all about).

The lack of experience goes hand-in-glove with motorcycle accidents. In Charlottesville, Virginia a study of cycle accident victims showed that 72% had received no operating instruction whatever.

A Vermont study revealed that 21% of accident-involved cyclists had been licensed less than a year. In California, this less-than-a-year group of cyclists had four times as many accidents as automobile operators in the same experience category.

The safest way to learn

The safest way to learn motorcycle riding is with the help of an experienced rider who has the interest and the credentials to teach you *safety* along with the basics of grip-twisting, lever squeezing, what to do with your feet, and how to lean instead of steer yourself through a turn. This does *not* mean your buddy down the block who roars around the neighborhood without a helmet, loves to do "wheelies" to impress the girls, and brags about threading in and out of home-ward-bound traffic at an average of five blocks per minute. This guy may still be alive, but it's *in spite of* the way he rides.

In many cities, there are organized safety instruction classes for beginners as well as those who have ridden awhile (long enough to know it pays to have some good advice). Ask your dealer, or your de-partment of public safety, about such courses. Some colleges hold motorcycle safety education workshops; ask for the instructor of safety education at your nearby colleges and universities. Several thousand high schools in the United States offer beginning motorcy-cle riders some kind of operator training and/or safety education.

In many states, the Department of Public Safety (highway patrol) conducts frequent motorcycle safety courses for anyone old enough to be licensed for operation, or who soon will be. In Oklahoma, for the smartest $10 investment any cyclist could ever make, state troop-ers present a comprehensive three-day course, furnishing the motor-cycle, the gasoline, insurance and training. No attempt to sell any make of cycle as being better than another is made; and features of many different makes are discussed during the training course.

This type of course, if available to you, is definitely worth your time, effort and money—and the certificate you receive at comple-tion is almost like a written guarantee that your chances of survival in traffic are increased 100%. Many of these courses and cooperative motorcycle safety organizations are new, so you can consider yourself lucky to benefit from them.

When I bought my first cycle, I was given a few minutes' explana-tion of ignition key operation, clutching, throttle and brakes, and al-lowed to circle the dealer's parking lot twice. Another suggestion or two followed on coordinating clutch and throttle, an admonition to watch those cars like a hawk, and some parting advice about simul-taneously gripping the clutch and hand brake levers (along with the foot brake action) if an emergency arose. With that, I was sent onto the street in front of the dealer's place of business and told to "get the feel" of everything in a round trip of a few blocks.

I was a good bicycle rider, so I was confident of my ability to balance; and I drive an automobile well in traffic, so I felt no fear. Actually, that "maiden" ride went pretty well; I even managed to negotiate a circle drive at another business down the street at my planned turnaround point, and then came to a respectable stop back at the dealer's. It was a lucky ride.

National statistics show that most motorcycle accidents happen within the first 500 miles of the rider's experience—often on his very first ride. So, if it's available, take a learner's course before you purchase your own bike. If not, read this chapter very carefully and heed the advice. More detailed information can also be had by writing to the Motorcycle Safety Foundation, 6755 Elkridge Landing Road, Linthicum, MD 21090. Ask for "The Motorcycle Rider Course." Perhaps you can get a copy locally through your motorcycle dealer.

Let the dealer deliver your cycle to your home, or ask an experienced rider friend to ride it home for you. Then take your time before trying it out. Read the owner's manual until you are familiar with the operational components of your bike *before* you go for a test ride.

Next, put your bike up on its center stand, to elevate the rear wheel. Sit in the saddle and reach all the controls with your hands and feet until you can close your eyes and touch them "by the numbers." Correct and comfortable posture—safe posture—means sitting square, leaning forward slightly. Good posture gives you more natural alertness, lessens fatigue and gives much-needed support to your kidneys. Your visibility is also improved by good posture—reason enough without any other considerations. In cycling, your position on the saddle will depend on your comfort and the speed at which you ride. In street traffic at moderate speeds, as in highway travel, move back on the seat for better road traction.

Still on the center stand, run through the start up, gearing and braking operations. Avoid any sudden moves that might disengage the center stand and take you and your new steed up the garage wall, or into the street. Be sure your bike is in neutral when starting. If there is no green neutral indicator light on either instrument dial, just check the rear wheel. It will roll easily in neutral, and be locked when your bike is in gear. If you kick start, use a good, sharp shoving motion with follow-through. Remember to fold the starter pedal back in after your start.

As you operate the ignition, clutch-and-gears, foot and hand brakes, horn, turn signals—"the works"—you'll begin to get the feel of it all. If some controls are awkward or inconvenient for you, ask your dealer to make these minor but helpful adjustments. There will be no charge if he sold you the bike. Be sure all lights work properly and are correctly beamed.

For your actual training runs, make use of a large shopping center parking area at a time when very few vehicles are around. Other good training locations include schoolgrounds and school parking lots during vacation months or on weekends (get permission first). Certain areas of your local fairgrounds and big industrial firms provide big parking areas which might be accessible to you during nonworking periods (Sundays, holidays, etc.). If you possibly can, let an experienced cyclist ride your bike to your training ground, then observe you and make firsthand suggestions on correcting your technique.

The buddy push

At your level practice ground, a good first move would be to straddle your bike, take it off the center or kick stand, put it into neutral and walk with it, motor off, until you control it well. If you did bring a friend along, he can provide one further intermediate step by pushing you while you are in the saddle (still with motor off) to give you the feel of balancing the bike with your feet on the pegs.

When you do start the motor to practice with power, keep your eyes ahead and release your clutch lever gradually, easing back on the throttle simultaneously. Don't be discouraged if your first few attempts are too jerky and kill the motor; it's par for the course, and the reason you're practicing. Keep in mind you can always go back to your starting situation by simply squeezing the clutch lever, taking your bike out of gear.

While you are learning to ride, you may want to glance at the neutral indicator light as you run through the gearing operation. Notice the definite difference in feel in your gear pedal when you hit neutral. Before long you will be able to identify neutral this way, without looking for the light.

As you practice, think through a complete maneuver before you actually perform it. Be content at first with startups, short straight-line runs, and smooth, well-coordinated stops. Keep your knuckles up as you ride; and during your practice miles, rely almost entirely on your rear (foot-operated) brake. That hand brake is deceptively powerful, with a positive and immediate effect on your "steering." Take your time in learning to use it, and don't touch it in a turning operation until you have it mastered.

During your straight runs, practice the full range of shifting, up and down. (The gear pattern I will be referring to in this book— "up" into high gears and "down" into low gears—is the most common. If your cycle is one of those with an opposite pattern, then your first, or "low" gear will be engaged by toeing *up*, and the other gears by pressing *down* on the gear pedal.) Keep your hands on the handlebar grips and away from the levers for clutch or hand brake unless you are actually gearing or braking. The same thing goes for your feet: keep them resting on the foot pegs unless you are in the act of gearing or applying your rear (foot) brake.

This complete practice shifting routine will give you a good feel of the speed that seems best for each gear change, and of the help your engine will give in slowing your cycle. When you can handle this smoothly, begin a straight run, gearing up. Come to almost a full stop using the rear brake/front brake combination, and gearing down as needed. Then without stopping, run back through your shifting to the top gear. In using both brakes in combination, the rear brake is applied first, followed closely by your hand lever squeeze that activates the front brake. In your practice gearing/braking runs, come to a full stop before you run out of straightaway, remembering to squeeze your clutch lever, and go into neutral. Then do it again. Go through similar combinations of up and down gearing, slowing and stopping, until the hand and foot movements begin to feel natural and easy.

The clutch/throttle coordination, which with practice becomes completely second nature, may prove a bit difficult at first. This may be due to the dissimilar mechanical hand movements involved: the left (clutch-grip) hand squeezes the clutch lever in-out while the right hand rotates the throttle-grip backward-forward, through an arc. As you squeeze the clutch lever for gearing, let up on the throttle. Then, when you have toed up or down into the gear you want, let the clutch lever return and simultaneously pull back on the throttle grip. When shifting to lower gears, decrease your throttle before engaging the clutch.

Find out at this point whether you can shift gears either up or down without clutching, and mentally file this away for possible future need. My first commuter bike shifted smoothly enough in a few gears without hand clutching, and the knowledge came in handy once when the clutch cable gave way. I was able to travel several miles to the dealer's service shop, with no clutch. (If you do have to resort to this, remember you will have to make intersection stops, and extra control is definitely needed when you start off in gear!)

Proper clutch, throttle and braking action

You only squeeze the lefthand (clutch) lever during gear changes, or to *briefly* neutralize the gear action. "Riding" the clutch will shorten its life, though there are times during spasmodic traffic flow when it is helpful to slip the clutch temporarily. Releasing your grip on the clutch lever allows the gear you have selected with your toe to engage. While you are learning to coordinate your throttle action, this clutch release should be smooth and deliberate. Time enough later to become the "fastest clutch in the West."

Downshifting as you approach a traffic light improves both your stopping power and your brake life, but beware engaging the gear so fast that you jerk yourself forward in the saddle. Always move into neutral as you come to an intersection stop. This not only prevents a premature jump into traffic, but also provides a needed take-off hesitation for shifting, enabling you to make sure no cross-traffic vehicle is stretching an amber caution signal with a last-second spurt at your expense.

You only rotate the righthand (throttle) grip backward towards you when you want to "give it the gas" and move out. Releasing your grip on the throttle has the same effect (on most bikes) as removing your foot from the gas pedal of an automobile; spring action automatically returns it to the idling position.

When you practice bringing your cycle to a stop at the end of a straight run, do it until you coordinate everything smoothly within a short distance with no fishtailing or skidding. Remember to start your braking with the foot pedal, followed quickly with hand brake levering. Above all, *do* squeeze your clutch lever when braking. If you need to gear down to assist in your slowing action, disengage the clutch (squeeze the lever) before your engine stalls.

If you have your cycle in motion and suddenly need to "set her down," simply grab and squeeze both hand levers at the same time, and coordinate the foot brake pedal. Remember, having done this and only this, your bike is still in gear the moment you release your clutch lever. Go into neutral; or into your first gear if you will be taking off again.

The kill switch

This is probably as good a time as any to bring up the matter of that red button or "kill switch." Your cycle is probably equipped with one, mounted on top of the handlebar alongside a grip. Its purpose is to provide a fast, hand-operation shutoff of the engine. It's for emergencies, and unless you have more than your share of those, it's an easy thing to forget. Periodically it's good to practice using that button, just so you will remember it's there and be prepared to use it in cases of throttle-jamming or other emergencies.

Normal reaction to a stuck throttle, of course, is to squeeze the clutch lever, hit the brakes and stop. But a flip of that kill switch can take you out of some panic situations immediately *if* you remember it's there. Some riders put this kill switch on the OFF position as a routine part of their lockup. This could help foil a thief *and* keep you aware of the button.

Being aware of the kill switch can save you some frustration and embarrassment, too. On several occasions through the years, whether accidentally or when a child has been fooling around my parked cycle, that red button has been tapped off its normal position unknown to me. I've spent a lot of time looking for some other source of "won't start" trouble before noticing that off-center switch.

How to turn and corner safely

When your observer friend can honestly rate your operation of all controls as being good on the straight runs of varying distances, begin to practice curves—wide, easy sweeps at first, then sharper ones, along with some figure eights. Go easy, because a lot of riders misjudge the amount of lean they can get away with while retaining proper balance. You *must* learn to feel how much angle of lean is safe, and how much would put you into an unmanageable sideslip. The surface condition has a great deal to do with this. A little sand or gravel can turn an otherwise easy curve into a quick put-down. Do your slowing *before* you get into the turn, and begin to resume your speed as you come out of the turn into a straightaway.

Keep in mind that you don't negotiate curves on a cycle by "steering" the handlebars—though it more nearly amounts to that at quite low speeds. You just *push down* on the handlebar grip on the side of the turn, and use controlled body lean. The *amount* of lean into the turn should be enough to negotiate the turn *and no more*. When you get the hang of it, it will be such fun you'll tend to overdo it; and overdoing a lean into a turn can have only an unhappy result.

After curves, practice cornering through imaginary intersections—some with no stop required, others complete with stop and start-up maneuvering. Be sure you practice cornering until you are 100% familiar with the principle of centrifugal force. If you find yourself cornering at a speed that begins to carry you into the right-hand curb as you turn left, or across the centerline as you turn right, simply *let up on the throttle* until your angle of lean corrects the problem. Take care, of course, not to reduce speed too fast, or you may flop your bike over right in the intersection. (If your practice cornering is confined to imaginary intersections, even such a "goof-up" will be much better than the real thing, in real traffic.)

While safe cornering or following a curve in the road requires slowing down in advance (with braking action, gearing down or both), you will need to practice simultaneous turning and braking for the sake of emergencies. Find your maximum ability in this regard, without losing control of your cycle or falling. Needless to say, this practice calls for extreme caution, with very gradual increases in speed and decreases in turning angle until you approach the danger point. Do *not* actually jeopardize your control. Just find out approximately where your "point of no return" is and resolve never to reach it in your street riding.

Moving into traffic

The operating maneuvers we've just covered deserve plenty of practice out of traffic. When you think you're really good out there in your no-traffic, wide-open parking lot, cautiously mix with low-volume traffic for further experience. Give other vehicles a wide berth, with as much separation between you as possible, while you are a beginning cyclist. In fact, you'll *never* be such a skillful rider (*nobody* is) that it would be smart to crowd a motorist, or try to rush him into a move he's being very deliberate about. Impatience is suicide on a motorcycle.

As you move from your initial practice ground into the stream of actual traffic, please remember *no one sees you*. So drive super defensively in the light of this paradox. Don't anticipate what you think a motorist is going to do, even if it appears to be perfectly obvious and the only logical move he could make. *Don't assume anything.*

In driving a car, you can anticipate logically and make certain reasonable assumptions. If you're wrong once in a while, you might dent a fender. But you're not driving an automobile now. You do not have all of that nice steel body protection surrounding you. For safety's sake, you must realize you're about as vulnerable as a pedestrian now, and act accordingly.

As to whether you should move into main thoroughfares or stick

with residential streets at first, I can't really decide for you. Personally, I stuck with the side streets for a couple of weeks before I ven-
tured forth onto the main traffic arteries only to find that for me,
they were actually safer in spite of the increased traffic. In those residential areas, I found speeders running yield signs with no compunc-
tion; sometimes even stop signs. In the main flow of traffic, they
seemed more orderly and cautious (odds are greater they'll be under
the watchful eye of the police there).

My first accident happened on the first day I rode to and from
work on my cycle. I had taken a residential street, and stopped at a
two-way stop intersection with no opposing traffic. I started up into a
left turn, and that turn kept getting wider and wider while I kept
getting more panicky, and finally went into the curb at my right
while *struggling* to stay in the street! Ridiculous? Sure it was. I
hadn't practiced enough before venturing into traffic!

I did not have all the moves in my mind and hands and feet as a
matter of second nature. A simple let-off on the throttle at the right
point would have made that turn very easy. But it wasn't my reaction, because it wasn't ingrained through sufficient practice. In that
instance, of course, it was a good thing that I had taken a little-traveled street. The same dumb caper in heavy traffic would have had
more serious results than a bent brake pedal, scraped fork, and
skinned shins.

So, when you are *sure* you've had enough practice to mix it up
with real, live traffic—*don't.* Go for another session, or two or three.
For the first six months or a year, the more you ride, the better you'll
get at it. After that, experience can either work *for* you, if you're in-
telligent, or make you overconfident if you aren't. The worst insurance risk in America is an overconfident cycle rider who is absolutely
sure he has "arrived," and nothing can happen to him.

Experience saves lives

Did I make a mistake in telling you of my embarrassment from that
first ride in traffic? Admittedly, I felt uniquely stupid about it until I
started checking the fatality records of our Highway Patrol headquar-

ters. I'm not unique. One 25-year-old who got on a 250 cc bike with no helmet and very little experience, sped through a residential section and did the same foolish thing I did. He failed to take an easy curve where the street just jogged a little to the right (that centrifugal force bugaboo again). But in his case, he ran completely off the street, down a six-foot embankment. His bike wound up in a culvert, and he was thrown off onto a mass of jagged rocks. Without a helmet, he died of head injuries. Safe-area practice experience on curves, coupled with a saner speed, could have prevented his death.

Another case involved a 15-year-old who had insufficient training, and hadn't had his new bike long enough to become familiar with it. He made the fatal mistake of failing to yield to a car on his right at an open intersection. (Driver Education before tackling a cycle would have taught him the importance of letting motorists have their right-of-way.) The car he tried to bluff out was driven by a 20-year-old girl with no driver's license because she was under suspension following a previous accident. She didn't bluff. The bike was laid down on its side before striking the car, and the boy didn't make it. With more riding experience and familiarity with his two-wheeler, he might have.

All too often, ignoring traffic laws results from cycling inexperience. The 25-year-old was speeding in a residential zone. The 15-year-old failed to yield. And in a third case, another young and inexperienced rider, with his younger sister a passenger on his overloaded 100 cc, was not only hitting 45 in a 35-miles-per-hour zone, he did it in the dark on a country road as he topped a hill. When he saw a cow in the roadway, there was no time to stop. The cycle skidded on its side just 18 feet after the impact, and the boy (who wore no helmet) died at the scene. His sister was badly injured.

The more experience you get on a cycle, the more you realize how easy it is to have an accident. And, if you're smart and want to live, the more cautious you become. In the last case history cited above, the cycle operator was only 14 years old, and had not taken time to practice and get safe experience before venturing onto a state highway. His 100 cc was unsafe for two riders; and riding double at his age is particularly hazardous in any event. He was illegally speeding; riding unsafely at night; was not alert or riding defensively; was taking a hill unsafely; and was not expecting the unexpected.

Each of these fatal mistakes is treated in a separate chapter of this book. But they are more than just words on a page; they are collections of life-and-death safety tips.

3. What Makes a Cycle Safe or Unsafe?

IF YOU BEGIN your motorcycling experience with a new machine, you can feel pretty good about its inherent safety. Most popular makes are well engineered and constructed. With the exception of the horn, which I will discuss later in this chapter, accessories are adequate and safe.

If you must limit yourself to a used cycle at the outset, take every possible step to check its safety. If a reliable dealer's service department will look it over for a small fee (just as you might have an expert mechanic inspect a car you are considering), it will be money well spent. Please don't entrust your life to the condition of your cycle unless you have a new one, or have obtained a "clean bill of health" for it from a disinterested third party who knows the specific make and model you are buying. A Maryland study showed defective cycles to be the number one cause of all motorcycle accidents.

Do the controls fit you?

When you sit in the saddle of your cycle, make sure the handlebars fit comfortably in your hands, with no forcing of the wrists. The two hand-lever controls (clutch and front brake) should be below your knuckles as you assume your riding position. The foot brake pedal should be positioned for quick and easy use, never above the level of your foot sole. Your gearshift pedal must be positioned for natural, comfortable toe movements in gearing either up or down. If any of these points are awkward or uncomfortable, have your dealer adjust them until they feel right; it's a matter of safety.

A few years ago, a 19-year-old rider decided to rev up his 10-year-old cycle to a speed of 60 miles per hour in a 35-miles-per-hour overpass zone in city limits. The age of his cycle can't be blamed for the fact that he crashed into a guard post and was killed. (I know a man who takes his 20-year-old machine onto the highways every year and has no trouble. He overcomes its age with constant professional maintenance.)

Don't tinker with safety

But the Highway Patrol report of this fatality contained four words that give us a probable cause: "substandard handlebars and fork." This simply means that somewhere along the line, the bike owner decided it would be fun to tinker around with some modifications that would demonstrate his customizing skill to his buddies. No sound engineering basis to tamper with the original design; just a chance to show some individualism.

The fact that handlebar control was no longer well-designed, but something that made operating the machine a bit tricky, may have made that rider's life more interesting—while it lasted. No doubt almost doubling the legal speed on that overpass also added a little "zest." But the result was hardly worth it. You'll have more fun living longer; *and* you'll have a better chance of that if you let the manufacturer do the engineering.

Safe tires

In the Maryland study previously mentioned, more than 11% of all motorcycle accidents were caused by tire blowouts. Don't assume from this that cycle tires are risky merchandise; they're not. But you *can* take it from this statistic that constant inspection of the condition of your tires is a must. Riding on tires you know are becoming smooth is nothing less than suicidal. Your treads can save you or wreck you anytime you take to the streets and encounter an emergency. When treads go down to 1/16th-inch depth, get new tires.

Keep them aired up to manual-recommended pressures, and use an accurate gauge of your own for frequent checks.

There is a definite difference in the tread design of street tires as opposed to the knobbies developed for dirt-bike riding. Again, the developers had good reasons for these design differences. For safety's sake, do your street and highway riding on street tires, not dirt-bike tires. Also, notice the tread difference on street bike front wheels as contrasted with rear tires. These opposing treads have been proven to give superior street traction, particularly on slippery surfaces. Don't monkey with them.

Good tire treads and good brakes go together in keeping you safe on two wheels. If your brakes are too slow or erratic in taking hold; or if they grab *too* fast, you're in trouble from the moment you take off.

Safe brakes

How do you feel about having both front and rear brakes? Like double protection? Do you think it might be O.K. to ride with just the front brakes (or rear brakes only)? A 15-year-old biker thought that was all right. He had rear brakes, so he took off with a pal his own age, illegal in itself, since he was licensed only for riding single. It was a dumb move anyway, because his 100 cc was never made for passengers, *and* he had no front brakes.

As if the odds weren't bad enough, this boy got up to 40 miles per hour at a crossing and tried to beat a freight train that happened to be going 55. The impact knocked the bike 63 feet, the operator 99 feet, and his passenger pal 102 feet. Both were dead at the scene. Who knows? With a full set of brakes, the boy might have tried stopping—and lived to be glad of the decision.

Being able to stop is simply an absolute necessity when you insert yourself into street traffic on two wheels. As you can see from the chart in Chapter 19, actual stopping distances for cyclists are greater than for motorists. This puts an even greater premium on good brakes and the practice of putting plenty of space between you and the car ahead. Otherwise, if the motorist has to make an emergency stop, you stand a good chance of ending up on top of his trunk deck or tangled up in his exhaust pipe.

As you ride, pay close attention to the efficiency of your brakes. The minute you lose some confidence in their condition, get them fixed by experts. Whatever the cost, it will be more than justified.

Safe lights

Working headlight, tail light, brake light and signal lights are also essential to your street cycle safety. If the manufacturer didn't include a set of lights as original equipment on your bike, it wasn't meant for street use. Get one that is "street legal."

When I first began riding, my bike was not equipped with the automatic switch that now turns on the headlight and tail light when the ignition is turned on. I tried to remember turning them on as part of my start-up routine, because a basic rule in street bike riding is to help others see you.

If your bike is too old to have the automatic "lights on" feature coupled with the ignition switch, either pay to have this done, or force yourself into the habit of always riding with your lights on, day or night. Statistics prove this saves lives. Of course, this only helps if your lights are really working, with good brightness. Check them out as part of your start-up routine, and don't forget to check for brake light reaction when you squeeze the hand brake lever or foot brake pedal. A strong battery charge contributes to cycle safety.

"Properly working" headlight means a properly beamed headlight. This needs to be checked at night. Keep in mind, too, that this beam level setting gets pushed out of place easily, so recheck it periodically. Turning signal lights may not be required by your state, but your own safety dictates their use. A working high-beam indicator light isn't essential, but when that bulb is operative, I find it easier to remain aware and show low-beam courtesy to other vehicles.

Rear-view safety

The National Safety Council says every motorcycle should be equipped with a rear-view mirror. I'll go further and say you need *two* good mirrors. My vision is excellent, but I have yet to find one mirror that will give me all of the rear-view panorama I need. With two, you can cover the wide left-right sweep you need to be safe during lane changes and be aware of vehicles entering your roadway from a driveway or intersection behind you. By *good* mirrors, I mean those of sufficient size and scan to get the job done—not a cutesy Maltese cross or other tricky design that gives you only part of the traffic picture you need. *Caution:* Viewed in your mirror, following vehicles appear to be farther back than they actually are. *Be alert to this fact.*

Effective horns

Why cycle manufacturers compound our safety problems with an ineffective "beep" for a horn, I don't know. It was one of my earliest disappointments with standard cycle features, and the situation hasn't changed. You've paid for my advice, now pay a little more for a better horn.

For about $30 you can get a dual air horn system complete with its own compact electric compressor. It hooks up to your present horn button, and really blasts off. I can tell you from personal experience, it will stop an 18-wheeler from pulling into the street from a driveway up ahead. It will even get through to a motorist enjoying the radio at his favorite decibel level: *loud.*

If this kind of horn saves your neck from a left turner just once, it's more than worth the investment. Picture yourself pulling to a stop behind a truck so wide you can't see either of his rear-view mirrors. The driver decides he stopped too far forward, and begins to back up. (After all, if you can't see his mirrors, he can't see you.) He simply believes he is backing a little nearer to the car behind you, and you're caught in a squeeze play. In such a fix and many more, you'll be very glad you invested in air horns.

If you still can't see spending even that much, at least put out $5 for a Freon horn, also mountable on most cycles. This type will give you about 200 blasts per can, and replacement Freon costs about $2. Get horn and Freon from the automotive/boating/cycle supplies section of your local discount house.

Warning: The air horn or Freon horn should *not* be purchased for the purpose of scaring little old ladies out of their wits, causing them to lurch into the car ahead. Nor is it funny to blast one behind a pedestrian in a walk lane and watch him jump into the cross traffic. Such shenanigans will get you a costly citation. You can control the volume with a quick tap when that's all you need, so be considerate. Also, be aware that it is illegal to equip a cycle with a siren, whistle or bell.

Reflectors increase safety

Street cycles should have reflectors visible from both sides, front and back. If a rear reflector is not a part of the tail light, you would do well to install one. Some diamond-design reflector strips come with adhesive backing for easy installation on any flat or nearly flat surface, and reflectorized tape gives you still further flexibility. The usual combination puts amber reflectors at the front and red at the rear. I installed a white (clear) reflector on each side at the rear, about five or six inches back of me, and just forward of the rear directional signals. Reflectors should be visible no less than 100 feet from your cycle, and preferably three times that distance.

Pre-ride inspection

The regular mechanical maintenance a motorcycle needs for safety begins with inspections that must become routine for you. Some working parts require frequent adjustment, and certain things need to be checked each time you ride. Others can be inspected on a periodic basis. Use your owner's manual as the guide for what is proper. If you don't have a manual, get one from your dealer and keep it with your cycle.

Each Time You Ride—
1. Check the power chain for proper tension and lubrication. As a rule of thumb, the chain should have approximately 3/4-inch of slack when you are in the saddle and your bike is off the kickstand.

2. Make sure both front and rear brakes are working properly.

3. Check the tires for proper inflation, good tread depth, and inspect for cuts.

4. Check your cables (clutch, throttle, hand brake) for possible fraying, looseness or crimped condition.

5. Make sure all lights (including brake light) and horn are working.

6. In your first block of actual riding, make sure clutch and throttle both work smoothly.

Many authorities recommend checking your oil and fuel levels before each ride. My own feeling is that a knowledge of your machine's mileage performance, coupled with reliance on your trip mileage register, will keep you aware of how many miles you can go without needing to refuel. I would recommend that you get gas as soon as it is convenient after switching to your reserve tank. This is equivalent to gassing up a car before you get down to a quarter-tank, the good habit of people who never run out of gas. *Be careful not to spill gasoline on a hot engine!*

If you are within a few miles of the point where you will need to switch from main tank to reserve, go ahead and turn the valve before taking off. It may keep you from having to perform that little function while moving (though you should be able to do this safely), and it will retain a bit of mileage in the main tank should you need it later.

Periodic inspection

As for the oil check, I look at this as a periodic inspection rather than something that needs to be done each time you ride. This is only true, of course, if your cycle is in good condition and not an oil burner. If it *isn't* in good condition, pre-ride inspections won't make it safe, *repairs* will.

Periodically (per manual schedules)—

1. Check oil level in both transmission and crankcase and add if required. Change oil per manual. Clean oil filter.

2. Lubricate power chain and adjust tension if too slack. Check for wear.

3. Test the handlebars for smooth turning in both directions, without noticeable "play" in the stem.

4. Test both side and center kickstands and springs to make sure they work readily, yet provide secure support and present no riding hazard. (If your kickstand is too loose, your cycle when parked may fall with little provocation. There should be good clearance when kickstand is stowed.)

5. Check for nuts and bolts that may have worked loose since your last periodic maintenance check. This should include all mechanical and electrical connection points.

6. If oil drips show up on your home-base parking, or if oily grime accumulates anywhere on your cycle, check for leakage sources and have them corrected.

7. Check battery fluid and keep all cells at proper fill level, with plates covered.

8. Wash your cycle when it needs it, or every six to eight weeks "whether it needs it or not." Wash with ignition key in place (OFF position).

9. After washing, lubricate pedals and power chain. Take up chain slack if needed.

10. Check clutch and hand brake levers for smooth operation, then lubricate and adjust cables. Compare your idling speed in neutral with clutch engaged, against engine speed when shift is in gear with clutch disengaged. It should be the same in both cases. If not, get clutch drag repairs.

11. Check rear brake and adjust if needed. Replace brake shoes as needed.

12. Tighten wheel spokes and check wheels for absence of wobble and proper alignment.

13. Drain and refill shock absorbers and front fork oil.

14. Adjust, repair, clean, and replace all lights and covers as needed.

15. Check all electrical wiring for worn insulation, faulty connections or loose ends.

16. Clean, regap or replace spark plugs.

17. Inspect and clean air cleaner. Replace as needed.

18. Lubricate throttle and check cable for adjustment.

19. Check mirrors and tighten in best position for optimum rear visibility.

20. Check carburetor and adjust idling speed.

21. Check and clean fuel tank, fuel valve strainer and fuel lines.

22. Check exhaust pipe and muffler. Remove carbon and retighten clamp bolts.

23. Check oil pump and adjust control level if needed.

If you have doubts about your mechanical ability, leave the more complex maintenance matters to your dealer's service department. Your safety is more important than the money you might save with questionable do-it-yourself operations. An annual overall checkup by a reliable dealer's service department is worthwhile, even if only to confirm your own maintenance expertise and give your bike a clean bill of health.

Emergency measures

In spite of a rider's best maintenance practices, it's well to know what to do in case the throttle sticks or the clutch cable breaks. These are two emergencies that do arise, which are never anticipated. In either case, *hit the kill switch and apply both brakes.* Keep in mind, of course, exactly what the traffic situation is when you hit your brakes; you don't want to wind up as a hood ornament. But you *do* want to regain control immediately. And, if the throttle sticks, you've got to shut off that runaway power. Get out of the traffic flow as swiftly as possible.

Engine problems

There's another kind of power problem with motorcycles: when your engine won't generate any, or you experience a power loss. Assuming the engine did start, you can check the spark plugs and look for either a clogged muffler or leaking head gasket. If it doesn't start, be sure you have gas and that the valve is ON—and that both the ignition switch and kill switch are ON.

Problems carrying passengers and cargo

You'll find in Chapter 10 why I consider passenger carrying hazardous. But the chances are high that you will carry a passenger, at least occasionally. So, let's at least be reasonable and agree that your cycle must have the necessary size and fittings for the purpose. It must handle the extra weight with fairly normal response in the controls. If you are a beginning rider with a bike no more than 125 cc, you'll probably have to violate the law to carry a passenger. And aside from that consideration, cycles of that size are not engineered and constructed to carry two people. This means you deliberately take a chance with two lives when you ride double on that kind of machine.

One 17-year-old took a 12-year-old passenger for a state highway spin on a 125 cc. Part of the "fun" in a ride like that is to impress the passenger with just how fast those two wheels will turn. This operator managed to hit 55 miles per hour even with the extra weight, but about that time he lost some of his steering control—perhaps because his young passenger began to get fidgety. They struck a culvert, went airborne for 21 feet, slid another 75 feet and hit a telephone guy wire. The operator died there. The cycle traveled another 35 feet and ejected the passenger, who landed 20 feet farther on, also dead at the scene. You'd be surprised how often this accident happens to cyclists who ride double on bikes that just weren't meant for it.

If you think I'm trying to say reckless stupidity is a franchise of the young, forget it. One year earlier, a 56-year-old man invited a 14-year-old to ride with him on a 100 cc. He pushed that little cycle up to 50 miles per hour on a county road with no shoulders. Then the suspension failed due to the excessive weight load, a wobble developed at that fast clip, and the operator lost control. Thrown into a ditch, both riders were ejected. Fortunately the boy survived to spread the word to his pals about the danger of riding double on an undersized bike.

Cargo carrying on a motorcycle is another thing to approach with common sense and caution. Some things you can do with complete safety. Others create an unnecessary hazard. As a rule of thumb, you'll be O.K. with items you can put into a back pack (which I find the most convenient way to carry "lumpy" pocket objects such as billfold, glasses, etc., and other items like library books, mail and small store purchases). Even items you can secure with a stretch cord usually ride well, if they don't bang against your knees when cornering, or add too much weight.

Loads you *can* carry must be fastened to your bike, not just hung on it. Never let a tie cord hang loose; it could catch on a wheelspoke. I carry stretch cords with me at all times. They are very convenient for small packages. Usually I confine my cycle-top toting to dry, small, lightweight sackfuls. I place the sack atop my gas tank with the rolled top of the sack towards me. A stretch cord *between* the sack's contents and the rolled sack top then secures the whole thing just fine.

Larger items that may be in a box, I prefer to carry behind me, fastened against the grab bar with stretch cords hooked tightly around the directional signal chrome arms. Again, you *must* limit the size and weight of anything you carry on a cycle—front, rear or back pack—to common sense proportions. If it looks or feels silly, it's probably dangerous.

When using stretch ("bungie") cords, it may be your custom to loosen one hook-end, place the parcel beneath the cord and rehook. But while you're going through this routine, it's easy for the *other* end hook to come loose without being noticed. When you start up, you suddenly find your parcel sliding off while you shift gears. Normal reaction is to grab for the beefsteak or whatever, and the result can be disastrous. *Be sure it's secure!*

What about cargo-carrying accessories? Yes, you can find windshield fairings with handy storage pockets, chrome luggage racks to mount at the rear, and, of course, some saddlebag compartments that hold a lot and come equipped with their own reflectors. I avoid all of these for various reasons. You can do as you like, but please keep in mind that with some of these gadgets you can dangerously overload the rear of your bike, creating control problems the manufacturer didn't anticipate.

Added loads cause differences in turning, braking and acceleration. All of these become more difficult depending on the weight and stability of the cargo. Basically, carrying packages on a cycle boils down to this: if they're heavy or bulky, use a car or a truck. A motorcycle is made for riding, not hauling.

Problems with "choppers"

Another way for a cycle to become less safe in my judgment is through "modifications" the owner decides to undertake. This includes creating a "chopper," which just doesn't come that way from the manufacturer. Personally, I think that's because the manufacturers don't consider them safe. They aren't noted for passing up any reasonable money-making opportunities. Most of the dealers I have interviewed on the subject have the same opinion. Some don't think this at all, and say it's simply a case of too many individual tastes to be satisfied by a standard chopper design. But the majority say the chopper is unsafe, unreliable and hard to handle safely. As one veteran dealer put it, "Some cycles are to look at, and some are for riding. A chopper is something to look at."

For a case history on the subject, we can look at what was planned to be a pleasant Sunday afternoon ride on a state highway by a 28-year-old cyclist. His chopper had been customized from a 350 cc. An eyewitness to his accident claims the slant-fork went out of control in a strong wind, at about 45–50 miles per hour. The cycle hit a guard rail near the beginning of a curve, and traveled along the rail 51 feet from the first impact. "Due to extended fork," reads the official report, "it was hard to get back under control." The rider was thrown at this point, his helmet was torn off, and he died at the scene of head and neck injuries. The chopper continued another 64 feet on its own. Was the eyewitness right in his evaluation? I can't say, but it could be.

My own dealer's service manager told me, "Every chopper on the road is a home-made job—some of them by good mechanics who customize for a real bundle. But most I've seen are jerry-built and dangerous. Any time we work on one, I limit our test-riding to short runs in the parking area. I don't let my men take them out on the streets." You will, of course, make up your own mind on the question of customizing a street cycle into a chopper or any other modified version. For me, there are entirely too many hazards on the streets and highways already. I prefer not to risk creating any of my own.

Problems with unfamiliar cycles

One more brief point before leaving this chapter: *unfamiliarity* with a specific cycle can make it unsafe for you to ride, regardless of its condition or your experience. Even if I were the best rider in the world on my 200 cc commuter bike, I would spend some little time getting acquainted with a 1,000 cc before straddling it for a cross-country trip. Differences in weight, horsepower and performance make these two machines handle totally unlike each other. Even in the same capacity range, different manufacturers build varying characteristics into their products.

My point is to become familiar with a strange bike before you mix it up with traffic to any appreciable degree. And no matter how willing an owner may be, don't borrow a cycle you're unfamiliar with and expect it to handle "just like any other."

A 20-year-old borrowed a 900 cc bike and took off through a city's residential section at a high rate of speed, wearing no helmet. He lost control at 55–60 miles per hour after his foot pegs scraped the asphalt for 187 feet. The big cycle struck a utility pole, he was ejected through the air, and finally collided with a tree. Unfamiliarity with the borrowed bike almost certainly contributed to his death. The excessive speed may have felt like easy cruising on the 900 cc—a dangerous deception as it turned out.

Riding a number of different sizes and makes of cycles is fine, as long as you take time to familiarize yourself with the differences to be found in each. It makes good safety sense, and will make you a better rider.

4. Dress for Safety

ON A MOTORCYCLE, where you ride exposed to the hazards of the road, you need to take advantage of every possible opportunity to compensate for your lack of protection. Your operating skill is one compensating measure. Protective clothing, helmet and boots constitute another.

The helmet question

As far as I'm concerned, there is no question that the helmet is the most important and necessary item of personal equipment you can use for the sake of safety. Lawmakers in all fifty states have been confronted by vocal groups of cyclists who insist (1) they can't hear well when wearing a helmet; (2) a helmet reduces a rider's vision; (3) there's no proof that helmets save lives; (4) they've even "heard about" a guy who was strangled by the chin strap during an accident; and (5) anybody of age should have the freedom to make his own decision about whether to wear a helmet.

The National Highway Traffic Safety Administration has answered these claims, saying (1) "a motorcyclist wearing a helmet can probably hear as well as, or better than, a driver in a car with the windows closed. A Department of Transportation-sponsored study found that . . . helmets reduce the loudness of both the sound of interest and the motorcycle noise by an equal amount. Consequently, as long as the rider can hear the motorcycle itself while wearing a helmet, he or she can also hear any other sound with a favorable signal-to-noise ratio at least as well as a driver who does not wear a helmet." As to vision (2), "all helmets provided a field of view of more than 180°, well above the 140° used by state driver licensing agencies to screen out drivers with possible vision problems. Further, a skilled cyclist continually scans the environment, turning the head from side to side, and thus can attain a field of view well above that available to most car drivers." Answering objection (3), the report says, "During 1974, motorcycle deaths exceeded 3,200. More than *one-third* of the fatalities occurred in the *six states* without fully effective helmet laws." Do helmets *cause* injuries (4)? The NHTSA cites a 1977 American Medical Association report, "No valid evidence was found to indicate that helmets were responsible for head, neck and shoulder injuries." And about that question of "freedom of choice" (5), NHTSA calls it freedom to gamble that the cyclist won't be killed or permanently disabled—then makes the valid point, "*when* they die or become permanently disabled in a crash, their families and society as a whole must bear the tremendous economic, psychological and social costs involved."

But because of the hue and cry, more than half our states and many individual cities have decided that as a matter of law, and in the name of "freedom," the cyclists (at least those over 18) *can* decide for themselves. Why it's still illegal to attempt suicide, I don't know, because cycling without a helmet comes about as close to that as you can get. In my state, the legislators vacillated, and finally gave up trying to tell the belligerent motorcyclists they had to use helmets (except for younger riders).

A 30-year-old man with no helmet was riding a 90 cc trail bike when he lost control in a curve and went down in the path of an oncoming car. There were 54 feet of scrape marks following impact, and the cycle rider was D.O.A. of massive head injuries.

Wearing a helmet, by the way, does little good if you forget to buckle the strap. I've started out that way a few times, and I immediately pulled over to the side to correct the oversight. Then I gave myself a bit of "inside talk," because I obviously started a ride with a good deal less than the proper mental alertness. A couple of years back, a 43-year-old tried to take a curve at 55 miles per hour. He went off the highway and was ejected when his cycle hit a rock. He lost his helmet and his life because he had failed to fasten the chin strap: As soon as you put a helmet on your head, *fasten it!*

I believe I've heard about all of the anti-helmet arguments, including the one that goes, "A helmet might just keep me alive as a cripple; I'd rather die!" Well, if you're going to play odds like that, you might as well do your thing. I really think those who decide to wear a helmet will be the ones with something in their heads worth protecting.

There are even some who cite statistics as a reason to ride without a helmet. Most of the riders killed and injured, they say, are wearing helmets at the time of their accident. I don't doubt that. But, most cyclists who never have an accident, or who escape injury and death in one *also* wear helmets. Most cyclists still wear helmets, period. But if our legislators continue to relax the rules on this vital issue, these facts will change. If ever the majority of our riders eliminate the practice of wearing a helmet, you can rest assured most of those who suffer injuries and death will *not* be wearing a helmet.

One statistic *is* reliable: the most common of all injuries to cyclists is the head injury; and about 80% of cyclist deaths are caused by injuries to the head. The Newhouse News Service reported in August 1977 that in 1966—the year before federal standards were adopted favoring mandatory helmet usage—there were an official 11.7 deaths per 10,000 registered cycles. By 1975, when all but three states had mandatory helmet laws, that rate had fallen to 5.1. When the state of Washington enacted legislation requiring the use of helmets, motorcycle deaths decreased 49%.

I realize many who read this book will be turned off by my attitude concerning the use of helmets; and you still have the privilege of riding without one. But my purpose in writing this book is to help you survive in traffic on a motorcycle. To me, that includes riding with a good helmet (one with a label showing SHCA, ANSI Z90.1, or Snell approval) securely fastened, and a good clear visor with lots of peripheral (side-view) vision capability built in. If you carry a passenger, provide a helmet—a spare, not your own. Insist that no matter how "brave" or "independent" he or she may be, the helmet has to be on and fastened before those rear pegs are flipped down.

If you like a dark visor for riding in sunshine, and it seems kinder to your eyes, equip your helmet with one. But for all night riding, use the clear visor only. The full-face protection a good helmet visor gives you against eye injuries, or face stings from rocks, bugs and blowing sand is another good reason to wear a helmet. Goggles won't give you the same protection; nor will a windshield. I have yet to find a helmet visor that won't become badly scratched after a time, despite the best of care. When glass cleaners fail to restore yours to respectability, discard it and snap on a new one. Every time you ride, you bet your life on your eyes.

Footwear advice

Over-the-ankle leather boots of the heel type, and preferably with rubber soles, will give you the kind of foot protection you need while cycling. The heels help position your feet firmly on the foot pegs, and the rubber soles give you better street traction and control of brake and gearshift pedals. This can be important to your comfort in such situations as holding on a steep hill, waiting for a light to change or traffic to clear. I admit to a personal preference for side-zipper boots that are dressier and faster to go on and off. Lace-ups probably give better ankle support.

Why boots? Simply more protection than anything else. If you wear shoes, *don't* wear tennis shoes, sandals or slip-on loafers. A thick pair of socks would give you about as much protection.

Protect your hands

Your hands are constantly working while you ride; and everything they do is vital. Give them the protection they deserve, with good leather gloves. I know what you are thinking: gloves are fine in the cold months, but silly in the summertime. That would be true if gloves only served the purpose of keeping your hands warm. Not so. They're a year-round means of protecting your hands from injury (knuckle bangs from rocks, etc.) and giving you a better grip on the handlebars.

I'll certainly agree that the kind of gloves you may need in winter months (thermal or other warm lining, and gauntlets to shunt off the chill breeze) aren't appropriate for other times of the year. You actually need two different pairs unless you have the same weather all year long.

Those light, short-cuff leather gloves for warm months fit well and give you comfort that keeps your hands from tiring early. Get gloves that are manufactured for the cyclist; others won't fit or protect as well. When you see a rider with well-protected hands, feet and head, you're looking at someone who is as interested in safety as in having fun—the mark of a good rider.

Clothing advice

Between helmet and boots, there is room for a wide variety of protective (and some sharp-looking) clothing. If you've never heard about "leathers" in connection with cycling, the reference is to long pants and long-sleeved jacket, both actually made of leather for the greatest possible protection on a motorcycle. You can take a spill and slide along the pavement in leathers, and come out with your skin intact. The same accident could cost a lot of skin, blood and misery if you were wearing no more than a short-sleeved shirt and permanent-press slacks. It's a case of the cow's hide saving yours.

I must confess I have never owned a set of leathers. But on more than one occasion, I would have been much better off with them. When I first heard about them, I visualized some very ugly, bulky garments. Don't make that mistake. They are soft, colorful and well-styled.

What I *do* wear (and this is a safe clothing minimum) is a long-sleeved jacket that has a zip-in quilted lining for cold weather. It buttons up high at the top above the front zipper, has tight-fitting elastic cuffs, features two big-capacity zipper pockets in the jacket and a handy inside pocket in the lining, and has reflective striping that helps motorists spot me quickly.

I also wear long pants of good material, and take care not to have flared legs or floppy cuffs that can catch in an embarrassing way at several points on my cycle. Your dealer will also have some nice one-piece jumpsuit type garments designed especially for the motorcycle rider. They're probably the next best thing to leathers for safety plus good looks.

Light, bright colors for your clothing helps make you visible. This fact has been extended to encompass light-reflecting vests or jackets, and reflectorized tape that can be applied to helmet, gloves and clothing as well as your cycle to add to your safety. Use the taping that is made for the purpose, and don't try painting fluorescent colors onto your helmet. Some paints will actually deteriorate the protective characteristics of the helmet material.

5. Physical Fitness Counts

ARE YOU IN GOOD HEALTH? Consider yourself physically fit? Pretty fair athlete? Or are you subject to dizziness? Spend a lot of money on doctors and medicines? Are you "accident-prone"? Clumsy? Rather uncoordinated? Never cared for sports because you weren't good at any of them?

If you had to answer "No" to the first three questions above, or even paused thoughtfully before answering "I think so," you won't be the best safety risk riding a motorcycle. As for the latter four questions in the paragraph, answering "Yes" or a reluctant "I guess that's a fair statement" should bring you around to the same conclusion.

Of course, answering the other way is no guarantee of your safety on two wheels, but the odds are stacked better for you. *Physical fitness counts* in cycle safety, as well as mental and emotional fitness.

That's because operating a motorcycle safely in traffic is difficult, downright challenging, in fact. Let's have no illusions about that. Being an excellent bicyclist is a good plus for you, particularly because it means you have that all-important good sense of balance. Being a very capable automobile driver is a plus if you are a good defensive driver with a perfect or near-perfect accident record. Otherwise, it means little. After all, in a car with automatic shift, coordination is relatively unimportant, and your balancing ability is meaningless. In a car you can and do take your eyes off the road and even the surrounding traffic at times, usually without any great risk if it's just for a quick glance at a billboard or a pretty girl.

But on a street cycle, your safety requires nothing less than constant attention, complete alertness and outstanding coordination and balance. You can do these things without too much regard to your age (up to a certain point), but you can't depend on doing them if you are physically unfit or subpar. If you don't trust your own evaluation of your fitness, get a thorough checkup by your family doctor and tell him why you want it. If he seems interested only in lecturing you about the many horrible emergency cases he's witnessed as a result of motorcycle accidents, tell him you're reading this book and intend to take its advice. It will help him be more objective.

There are some physical conditions not compatible with safe cycling. I'm not talking about such obvious things as blindness or having only one arm, but rather such conditions as the following.

Vision problems

The ability to face straight ahead and distinguish objects and actions to the right or left of your body within reasonable distances, is the mark of good peripheral vision. It is very helpful to cyclists. By the same token, poor peripheral vision is a liability. This doesn't mean you can't ride a motorcycle safely, but it *does* mean you'll have to compensate for the fact when you ride. Fortunately, all that's required is for you to twist your neck a little more often, to scan in a more direct fashion what's taking place to your right or left. If you have good eyesight, including above-average peripheral vision, you are fortunate.

Hearing problems

Compensating for poor hearing is done in the same way you make up for poor peripheral vision. Keep your head moving to know what's going on around you. Keep a sharp eye on your rear-view mirrors for a telltale flashing red light approaching—and up ahead for the same thing.

Dizziness

Everybody feels a little woozy once in a while. But if you are subject to frequent dizziness or fainting spells, better forget cycling. Otherwise, if you suffer a little dizziness while cycling, pull over at the first convenient and safe spot, and rest until you are sure it has passed. If it happens before you start, postpone your trip for the same period of time. If you're hungry, stop and enjoy a good meal. The rest and the food will both be good for you.

Alcohol and drugs

It seems incredible to me that anyone would "drink and drive" on a motorcycle, or relinquish control of faculties to drugs and do the same. But some do. Motorcycle fatality records are liberally sprinkled with instances, all too many of them involving young riders. What can I say? It's *suicidal*. And, if suicide is your objective, please reconsider; life is beautiful.

In a college town, a 25-year-old was speeding 55 miles per hour in a 30-miles-per-hour zone. He suddenly swung his big cycle left of the centerline into the path of a pickup that was also coming too fast. The cycle operator, who not only had been drinking but also carried a few lids of marijuana, stayed with the bike 96 feet before being ejected in an impact on the shoulder of the wide street. His body wound up 160 feet away.

Let's face it: all your life you've heard "if you drink, don't drive." And drug use has as its primary objective getting "high" and "spaced out." What that really means is being out of your ever-lovin' gourd. And if I have to inform you that such a condition is unsafe for operating a cycle, you're already out of it.

Alcohol, abuse-type drugs, even certain prescribed medications (pain-killers, muscle relaxants, etc.) that produce temporary side effects, will give you a false sense of well-being. At the same time, your concentration will suffer, your reaction time will slow down dangerously, and your vision, space perception and judgment will be seriously impaired. In such a condition, operating a motorcycle is completely foolhardy. If you have an accident under such circumstances, you will not only be responsible for your own fate, but perhaps that of others as well.

Emotional stress

More than once when I've been angry at someone or something, I've been tempted to jump on my cycle and cruise away, if only for a mile or so. A few times I've started; but reason soon prevailed. That is no time to risk life and limb without the concentration so necessary to safe riding. And if you are experiencing any strong emotion such as anger, despondency—even jubilation—you are apt to find it very hard to ride with the observant and calculating coolness needed for maximum safety. Wait until you have "calmed down," or ask a friend to drive you. (Even driving a car at such times isn't safe.)

Leg cramps

If you're young, you may have no problem with these. If you're not, a few fast sets of tennis followed by a cycle ride home in a cooling breeze can induce a bad case of muscle cramps. Whether it's in your leg, or a "charley horse" in a foot, it's definitely incompatible with safe operation of a motorcycle. Pull off and get rid of the condition before moving on—the sooner the better. A fierce cramp can become a pain-filled band as hard as steel in seconds; and using such muscles to operate cycle controls is out of the question.

Fatigue factor

You can't be properly alert if you're all fagged out, from whatever cause. So try to do your cycling when you feel good. Incidentally, *poor posture* can contribute to fatigue and inalertness. When you ride, sit well on the saddle—straight and square, with a little forward lean. (If you ride perfectly erect, you may be too far forward in the saddle for proper weight distribution.)

Naturally, we don't need to tell you not to ride a motorcycle when you're sleepy, right? Wrong. Unbelievable as it may seem, people do it—though usually not very long. Case in point involved a 36-year-old who liked to take his 900 cc cycle onto the highways for real trips of varying distances. Visiting his brother on one of these junkets, he stayed until 4 A.M., then simply refused to stay the rest of the night. He actually stayed awake another 2-1/2 hours, tooling along in the night breeze on his homeward journey. But at 6:30 A.M. he fell asleep, hit a bridge abutment, went airborne for 60 feet, then his body traveled another 30 feet and came to rest in a private drive. Had he rested earlier, this final one might have come many years later.

Heart problems, arthritis, and epilepsy

If you have a real history of heart problems, check your state law as to your eligibility. Even if you get the state's O.K., counsel with your physician and at least limit your cycling according to his advice.

If you have a bad, chronic arthritic condition, cycling won't be safe—particularly if it's your hands that suffer most. They really get a workout on a motorcycle. If it's an occasional condition, cycle on your trouble-free occasions.

Same suggestion for those with epileptic conditions as for those with heart trouble. Personally, I wouldn't take the risk.

6. How to Avoid Surface Hazards

FROM YOUR FIRST solo trip, for as long as you ride a motorcycle, the surface you're riding on will have tremendous importance to your safety. You are not a dirt-bike rider out for thrills. You are in the business of getting from one place to another, economically and all in one piece.

Different communities take different care of their streets and thoroughfares. The same is true of the maintenance given roads and highways by counties and states. And even the best maintenance crews can't be everywhere they might be needed, all the time. Chuckholes and other hazards to cyclists will develop, and they are much more hazardous to you than they are to motorists.

Familiar routes

In view of this, it is vital that you *know* the condition of the surfaces you travel. If you use your cycle primarily for transportation to and from work, it will pay you to take the same route every day. You may consider this monotonous, but it will pay off in safety. You should memorize surface conditions for the entire route, knowing when to slow down and what to avoid. You should also become familiar with the "rhythm" and character of the traffic flow on that route at the hours you are using it.

You should learn where to expect traffic to enter a main artery from a side street, where motorists entering or crossing your street are forced to look into the sun, or where they approach a stop sign partially hidden by overhanging limbs, hampering their vision. You should even learn where to look out for the Great Dane that enjoys chasing cyclists and automobiles. (A dog can wreck a cycle, whether or not he is chasing you. Just chasing a cat unexpectedly across your path can create a real hazard.)

Unfamiliar routes

O.K.; it's smart whenever possible to stick with a familiar route. Obviously you can't do this all the time. This simply means you need to slow down and be especially alert when you ride a new street or highway for the first time. This is so important to me, I have developed a little "ritual" for such times. The moment I ride onto an unfamiliar route, I consciously say to myself "Unplowed ground!" occasionally as I proceed. You can change the words or adopt some other method if you prefer; this works for me. In consciously re-

minding myself that I am riding on an unfamiliar surface, I sharpen
my eyes and reflexes even more than usual, to avoid an unexpected
hazard. I recommend some such technique to you.

Let's take a look at some specific conditions that cause surface
hazards, and discuss ways to cope with them.

Rainy surfaces

Rain presents an automatic danger to cyclists. I take my car when it
has rained, is raining, or obviously soon will be raining. Wet, slippery
surfaces make it much more difficult to stop or maintain your balance. Because motorists also have a lot of trouble in the rain, the
odds against your safety really zoom.

You've seen plenty of "Slippery When Wet" signs; if you really
want to know what they mean, just go about "business as usual" on a
motorcycle when it first begins to rain. This is the most dangerous
time of all, before the rain has had a chance to wash away the surface
dust, grease and other foreign materials that have accumulated. During this early time, all these surface contaminants are loosened and
mixed with water to form a very slippery point of contact. Later,
mud gets carried onto the pavement by trucks; this is also a hazardous combination to cycle through.

What can you do if you are caught in the rain? *Reduce your
speed,* and *increase your caution.* Avoid wet, painted lines (slick
when wet), manhole covers, puddles or pools of water that present an
extra hazard and may hide a chuckhole, traffic lane centers (often
oil-coated, especially dangerous when wet), and even wet leaves,
which are deceptively slick. Keep your bike upright, with minimum
lean on turns. Accelerate and reduce your speed gently and gradually. This calls for increased scanning of the road surfaces ahead, to
have maximum advance warning of a required stop.

If the rain is bad, your vision will also be less than safe, and you
need to find a sheltered spot to wait out the storm. If you are on an
unpaved road, mud and ruts will add to your danger. Pull off and
wait. One 14-year-old on a 250 cc failed to take this precaution, and
paid with his life. The county road he traveled after dark was muddy
and deeply rutted. Evidence at the scene indicated he was riding at

an unsafe speed, and was thrown from his cycle by the ruts. He had too many hazards working against him.

If you are forced to ride through water, check both sets of brakes afterwards to make sure they are still in working order. You'll want to be clear of traffic before doing this, and apply your brakes *gently.* If there is no response, keep applying light pressure in areas free of traffic until your brakes dry out properly for safe stops.

Ruts and mud

Motorcycle tires are of a different design from those on the so-called "dirt bike." They are basically designed for hard-surface riding; and even on dry, well-maintained dirt roads their performance is inferior to that of dirt-bike "knobby" treads. The going gets rougher when you take on a dirt road that is dry but rutted. Either deep sand or a muddy, deep-rutted road should be considered impassable on a street bike—and hazardous for *any* cycle. There are a few adjustments you can make in your steering, the distribution of your body weight, in throttle control, the gears you select and your use of the clutch that help in snaking through deep mud and sand. But the purpose of this book is teaching you how to stay alive in traffic on a motorcycle. I really have no desire to help you combine traffic and dirt road hazards. Nothing I could tell you would help that much. On a street bike, stick to the hard surfaces.

Ice and snow

Wet streets are bad; streets covered with snow and ice are disasters. Stop a minute to think about that sinking feeling in the pit of your stomach that comes when you try to gently "feather" your automobile's brake pedal at an icy intersection, only to glide uncontrollably into a hubcap-wrenching impact with the curb above the storm sewer. Or to slide into a body-crunching collision with a big new luxury car, as if you had a real need for higher insurance premiums.

Well, that's the kind of experience you can have with four wheels during any typical winter. On a motorcycle, venturing forth at such times is sheer madness. You could be a professional tightrope walker and still have a balancing deficiency on such surfaces. That's why the

Motorcycle Safety Foundation says simply, drivers "must avoid operating when traction is insufficient for proper vehicle control." And believe me, if there is ice and snow on the streets, that's "when."

So park your bike until the streets are dry, and remember that even when the street in front of your home looks just fine, the overpass bridges can be dangerously icy. And that an isolated patch of ice no bigger than a basketball backboard could be your downfall—literally.

Dry but slippery surfaces

Slower speeds and extra caution are also required on surfaces littered with sand, small grit or loose gravel. You are so much more apt to lay down your cycle in a turn on this kind of surface, it really should be a part of your early practice, just to get the authentic feel of the problem. Go to your parking lot with a medium-sized grocery sack filled with sand, and scatter it over a yard-wide circle. Then *cautiously* ride across it in a *very slight* turning move. Let me emphasize the *very slight* turning maneuver. You're not out to damage your bike or scrape your shins, but to see for yourself how easy it is to lose your traction on this kind of surface. It will teach you respect for good surface conditions in a hurry.

More recently than I care to admit, I went down in a cautious, low-speed U-turn. I had seen an area of dust on the street surface, but I completely underestimated its capacity to skid my tires right out from under me. In turning operations on *any* but the cleanest, driest surfaces, you can't be too careful. (Another truism involved here is that you will invariably damage your cycle in an amount just under your insurance deductible. *Uncanny!*)

These dry, loose surface materials increase the distance required for stopping, just as surely as a wet surface. Riding on such surfaces is an "easy does it" matter if you care about safety. By all means, reduce your speed drastically or be prepared to learn the hard way why the Motorcycle Safety Foundation calls these "quick-spill" materials. Keep in mind that 99-44/100% of your street surface can be perfectly dry and safe; but you can still be tripped up by a sandy patch precisely where you are forced to make an emergency stop. The only remedy is constant surveillance of the surface you're traveling, and a sane speed.

The University of North Carolina Highway Safety Center made a study of single vehicle motorcycle accidents in that state. According to its data, the most serious road defect in 7% of such accidents was loose materials on the road surface. You will avoid more of these traction-destroying materials if you stay off the shoulders.

Metal surfaces

Metal objects on your riding surface, such as manhole covers, gratings and railroad tracks, are slick enough to limit traction. Avoid them when you can. Otherwise, take them straight on (90° angle approach to railroad tracks) and move across at a reduced speed but without hesitating.

Taking railroad tracks as nearly as possible at a right angle means that if the tracks themselves are at an angle with your riding lane, you will arc your cycle to set up properly. As you approach the crossing, swing your bike roughly parallel with the tracks, then turn to cross at the right angle. At some point in this maneuver, you will find yourself moving closer to the adjacent flow of traffic. Take care (1) not to get *too* close to other vehicles; and (2) not to confuse or startle motorists in the surrounding traffic by your maneuver. True, a good automobile driver will be aware of what you are about; but many will misunderstand. Some will even think you are one of those dodging, weaving nuts. Whenever possible, then, gauge your approach speed such that no motorist will be close to you when you move to cross the tracks at the safe 90° angle.

Broken paving

A recent "spell" of 100° weather caused one of our concrete interstate highways to buckle, leaving a 12-inch bulge stretching across part of the road. Before the problem was reported and barricades were erected, more than a dozen vehicles hit the bump hard, with flat tires the gentlest result. Can you imagine what would happen to you on a cycle if you collided with that foot-high chunk of concrete at high speed? Watch your riding surface—and don't speed so fast that you can't avoid a hazard clearly visible.

I hope you haven't decided to forget this particular bit of advice because temperatures are more moderate in your part of the country. Other factors can produce the same buckled concrete hazard. For that matter, something dropped onto the highway or street from a truck can be just as dangerous. So, keep alert!

Broken paving can also take the form of chuckholes and cracks, which are equally as dangerous as buckled concrete or other bumps in the road. They may be *more* hazardous, because some are tough to spot until you are right on top of them. Experience will teach you the kinds of shadows on the surface that may indicate paving holes.

All obstacles of this nature are real hazards to the cyclist. Avoid them by going around them if you can; this is best done when you spot the obstacle in advance and have time to reduce speed. Veering at the last moment is probably at least as dangerous as hitting the obstacle. As in the case of making a turn or going into a curve, the time to slow down (by using the rear brake and shifting down a notch) is before you reach the hazard. *Do not* use clutch or brake while negotiating a bumpy or slick surface.

In taking a bump, get a firm grip on the handlebar, push your body up from the saddle, and hold yourself loose in the joints (knees, wrist, elbow) to more easily absorb the shock. Keep your feet on the pegs, and return to your supportive sitting position as soon as possible. When you stand on the pegs to take a chuckhole or bump, shift your weight back and take care not to let the impact cause a jerkiness in your throttle feed.

You may need to accelerate slightly as you cross a chuckhole. But, if there is loose material edging the hole, or if you have a question in your mind, *don't* accelerate. A certain speed that varies with the size of the hole will carry you smoothly across. This is a decision you'll need to make, and there will be little time to think about it. Remember, you can't get into these tough situations if you proceed with proper alertness as to your riding surface, and at a sane speed.

If you *do* take a good lick on the edge of a chuckhole, or unavoidably encounter other street surface hazards such as glass, debris, etc., pull over right away. Take the time to inspect carefully for any possible damage to tires, spokes, rim, etc.

Ready for a little safety quiz? Consider this fatal accident. A 40-year-old had done some work on his 750 cc cycle, and wanted to test ride it. He took it out on a sparsely traveled county road and got it up to 75–80 miles per hour. Suddenly a depression in the blacktop showed up, and he swerved quickly to the left. His machine struck on the left side, righted, struck on its right side, then flipped and rolled over, ejecting him to his death.

What did this man do right? Wrong? The only *right* move he made, as I see it, was to choose an isolated road for his test run. If it encouraged him to rev up to nearly 80 miles per hour, even *that* was a mistake. The safe way to proceed would be to run over a course of one or two miles at a low speed, checking out the surface condition of the road. Finding it safe, he might then push his speed up for a good test, say to 60 miles per hour. But blasting along at 80 without knowing about the hole was one fatal mistake. The other was trying to swerve left to miss the hole. A motorcycle can take a lot of punishment in a straight-on encounter. He should have tried it. Of course, that depression might have looked like a miniature Grand Canyon. The *key* mistake was an uncontrollable speed over an unknown surface, a deadly combination.

Grease and oil slicks

These hazards are quite common, particularly on older streets and highways that have had lots of time to accumulate deposits. They are especially bad when rain-slick, but should be avoided as much as possible at any time.

You can minimize your risk by riding to the left in an individual lane, away from the oil-coated center, and by choosing the legal lane with the least buildup from oil deposits.

Litter and debris

Road litter, broken glass and other types of debris that can interfere with a cyclist's safety are found everywhere, in spite of stiff fines by some states and communities, and the admirable national anti-litter campaign.

Protective measures you can take are, again, a good, constant eye-scan of the surface ahead, and the kind of sensible speed that gives you a chance to avoid the debris. You can't, of course, concentrate on the riding surface to the exclusion of traffic or things going on in your rear-view mirrors. But you *must* know what you will be encountering on the roadway ahead if you care to survive.

All in all, the heavily traveled regular traffic lanes are kept more litter-free than the shoulders. This is one more good reason to avoid riding there, tempting though it is at times. When you are riding with another biker, stick to the regular lanes. One on the shoulder is just asking for trouble. There's a greater litter hazard there, and also because a vehicle ahead might suddenly take to the shoulder and cause a collision.

Two 14-year-old friends were using the wrong method when the one riding on the shoulder hit some obstacle and was tossed over his handlebars into a roadside fence. Even though both riders were doing an easy 30–35 miles per hour, the boy who was ejected was dead on arrival at the county hospital.

Dips and bumps

As if chuckholes, bumps and cracks in the pavement aren't enough to worry the cyclist, other problems are built right into the roadway. A couple of the deliberately created problems are the street-width dips and raised barriers. The dips vary in depth and slope, and are intended to slow traffic for the benefit of surrounding property owners. It works well with those who know the dips are there; but almost invariably the warning signs I have observed in connection with these dips are placed about a block beyond the dips and after you have broken an axle.

The raised barriers occur in alleyways, parking lots, and in the street in front of some businesses. They are generally slanted upward about four to six inches to a rounded top. The intentional bump they give to vehicles is intended to serve about the same purpose as the dips, except for the benefit of commercial or governmental establishments.

Sometimes you can ride your cycle around the bump barriers; but it's best to simply reduce your speed and take the obstacle straight on. You can sit out the dip, but in riding over the raised barrier, stand up on the pegs and hold your arm and leg joints loose (but keep your grip firm on the handlebars).

Configurations that are not planned, but do present a hazard, include wavy or "washboard" asphalt, pavement edges that drop off dangerously to the shoulder, and misaligned pavement. These must be learned and avoided as a matter of becoming familiar with a traveled route. To keep out of trouble from such hazards the first time you encounter them, treat every unfamiliar route as potentially dangerous, and keep your speed down accordingly.

Bridges and guard rails

Both of these road features have from time to time given a lot of trouble to motorcycle operators. Both are necessary, and here to stay. If you stay far enough away from them while riding your cycle, the chances are you'll do just fine. (Yes, I do have my tongue in my cheek. This is like the advice my mother paid 25¢ for in the days when mail order schemes were less supervised, and quarters were hard to come by. Mom succumbed to an ad promising to reveal the "secret of how *never* to cut yourself." For her 25¢, she got one sentence of advice: "Never cut *toward* yourself; then you'll *never* cut yourself!")

My mother finally had to admit that was sound advice; and so is mine. Ride properly in your lane, at the right speed and with enough separation between you and guard rails, culverts or bridge "walls," and you have little to worry about. These are fixed structures that won't be running into *you.* Chapter 22 gives some facts about riders who got too close to various hazards including bridges.

Pets and people

Strictly speaking, I suppose these are no more properly considered "surface hazards" than other vehicles would be. But as an author's prerogative, this is the chapter where I choose to deal with them.

Part of the rationale for this decision is the fact that if a dog chases a cat in front of your motorcycle while you are riding blissfully down the street, it's that *surface* you'd better be watching. They become part of it with blinding speed; and woe to you if you're proceeding at a similar pace. Small animals can wreck large cycles, and cause the rider serious bodily harm. Also, there are certain dogs that have a real passion for chasing after bikers and nipping at their heels. *Don't kick out* at such a pesty pet and try to ride on at the same time. *Do* move on promptly; but not at the cost of colliding with a car you forgot to watch when the dog came at you. If you have taken my advice and have a set of air horns, they can startle a belligerent dog into beating a hasty retreat, and you'll thank me again.

Most dogs that chase give an early indication of their intention as you approach. It helps at times to gear down before you reach the dog, then power up swiftly to catch him off guard. But again, stay aware of the traffic situation as you make this maneuver. If it comes to a choice between a dog bite and tangling with a car, choose the dog. You'll live to sue its owner, and you can use the judgment money to get a new pair of sturdy riding boots.

Dead animals also pose a danger to cyclists. Keep a sharp eye out, particularly on road and highway trips. If your traffic condition permits, ride around them. If you see that your present speed will bring you to the dead skunk at the same time an approaching vehicle will be opposite you, change your speed and give yourself room to maneuver.

In some areas, livestock can roam at will alongside the highway. They can suddenly and unpredictably decide to come onto the highway; so proceed cautiously. Even where there is no legal "open range," an occasional cow or horse can get free and become your hazard.

As for those two-legged animals called pedestrians, give them all the right-of-way they want. Under the law, they have it anyway, as opposed to vehicular traffic. Give them a wide berth even when they are illegally "jaywalking." No exceptions. And just as the cats and dogs can and do dart out suddenly onto the street from behind parked cars, so do children and even adults at times. Stay alert!

My last point on this subject: motorists ahead, going your same direction, can see road surface hazard; you can't. When they do, they may stop suddenly and without warning. You need to ride capable of stopping just as suddenly; or if this would put you in a squeeze with a following vehicle, be ready to make the *right* move to one side or the other. Once more with feeling: *STAY ALERT!*

7. The Reckless Die Young

I DIDN'T take up two-wheeling until an age when most people begin to feel that *all* cycle riders are young, reckless idiots. And according to the American Driver and Traffic Safety Education Association, those most often involved in motorcycle accidents with injury or fatality *are* young and inexperienced riders.

In Oklahoma during 1978, 82% of the motorcycle accident victims were age 27 and under; over 26% were 16 or under. If you are under 25, you are about 16 *times* as likely to be killed while operating a motorcycle as you are in an automobile! I'm *not* saying don't ride a cycle. I *am* saying these are the facts. *You* decide how careful you have to be to avoid becoming a statistic.

In all fairness, most people who ride motorcycles *are* under 25. This fact influences the statistics I just cited. But it isn't just the young who do dumb things on cycles. Just a few years ago, a 32-year-old man took his 250 cc bike on a ride right smack down the middle of some railroad tracks! It was so bumpy and erratic, proper steering control was out of the question. So after he made it a mile away from the nearest road, he bounced against a rail and was unceremoniously dumped. Not into the soft weeds along the right-of-way, but on down the tracks, where his unhelmeted head got fatally bashed. It was a unique gamble; but one too permanent for my liking.

You can't do anything about your age; but you can be smart enough to eliminate the show-off, daredevil risk-taking that too often characterizes the young rider. If getting to be even a year older interests you, there's just no room in your cycling career for gambling in traffic, *period*.

To speed, dart in and out of traffic, and ride headlong into any situation where the odds are against you or completely unknown—these are *not* actions that classify you as a brave young hero. They give unmistakable proof that you are a senseless young candidate for a morgue tag. The guy who commands the greatest respect in traffic today is the one who knows that the shortest distance between two points is really by way of courtesy, patience and law-observing good sense.

My bluntness doesn't come from a lack of understanding young people. In my twenties, I did those foolish things, and managed to live only because I had automobile steel wrapped around me. If I had taken up cycle riding at that age, without the benefit of good training or advice, I'm sure I would never have survived. I took chances in a Model A Ford that would get me quickly into the obituary columns on a motorcycle.

Right "up front" as we get into the specifics of recklessness, let me say if you want to ride a motorcycle, *don't take chances*. If you want to take chances in today's traffic, rent an armored tank and leave the motorcycle alone.

Showing off

Recklessness—taking obvious and unnecessary risks—is very often a simple case of "showing off." It's an attention-getting device, and it usually achieves that result. Problem is, you can get killed in the process and the attention goes for naught. Like the 18-year-old on a 450 cc, with a 17-year-old passenger in a small rural community. These boys crossed the main downtown intersection from a standing start and performed a sensational "wheelie" at something over 50 miles per hour. The bike then went out of control across the center-line, into the path of a pickup truck driven by a 15-year-old girl. If she was the only one they were trying to impress, they probably succeeded. Their cycle crashed into her pickup, the operator sailed 50 feet through the air to his death, and the passenger flew 98 feet and suffered massive injuries. Showing off provided the cyclist's last performance; was it worth it?

Operator negligence

In its various forms, including inattention, negligence on the part of the motorcycle operator causes a high percentage of accidents involving no other vehicle. According to the Maryland motorcycle safety research study, operator negligence was the largest single cause of urban nonintersection accidents in this category. Other operator risks such as failure to reduce speed, and improper use of the road, also ranked high on the list of causes. To my way of thinking, all of these amount to recklessness.

Unfamiliar cycles

In Chapter 3, I mentioned that a cycle is actually unsafe for you if you've never ridden it or one like it before. Now I'll go further and say that until you take time to familiarize yourself with such a bike, it would be an unnecessary risk to simply hop on it and take it out for a spin. *Take time.* Very little is necessary if you already know how to ride; and the stakes are high.

As a Christian I believe in putting trust in my fellow man. As a motorcycle operator, I know that blind faith in others who make up the traffic stream around me is plain gambling with my life. The Automobile Club of Southern California made a study revealing that more than three times out of five, when autos and cyclists collide, the *motorist* is at fault. Now this may give you some comfort as to your chance of paying a fine after an accident, but it will be small comfort when you're a mummy in traction at your local hospital. The moral is, unless *you* make all the right moves, you're taking chances—and that's a safety no-no.

Following too close

Three-fourths of the time, statistics tell us, accidents between car and cycle are caused by the cyclist following too close. Pretty stupid way to ride, wouldn't you say? Keep two or three car lengths between you and the vehicle ahead when street traffic is moving moderately. You'll find it a lot harder to become an accident statistic if you give yourself this much separation, this much reaction time to potential emergencies.

I've already mentioned how vital it is to constantly scan the riding surface you're traveling. You just can't accomplish this most important job if you are following too close. You'll have enough trouble with motorists *behind* you who enjoy tailgating. Shake them as soon as you can; but meanwhile, be sure you've put enough space in front of you for some emergency maneuvering.

Riding between lanes

What about riding that nice dash-line between lanes of traffic going in your same direction? Plenty of room for two cars and a motorcycle between them, right? And the line itself serves as a riding guide for the cycle operator. What could be handier? And isn't it true that the California Highway Patrol has stated officially that this practice is not against the law?

That's right. California went on record as saying between-lanes riding by a cyclist would not get him arrested. And there may be other states that rule the same. But in the same breath they'll give you this hooker: *If* the cyclist is involved in an accident while riding this inviting zone, *he* will be cited, because he's there *without* any right-of-way.

If that sounds like legal double-talk, your I.Q. is O.K. Of course, the most potent argument against such a practice is that the zone itself is Dead Man's Alley. Nobody can see you as you zip blithely along where a right-lane driver can and will at any moment pull unexpectedly to the left in front of you, to check the passing situation up ahead. And where a left-lane driver will swerve to the *right* in front of you to avoid trash on the roadway, or prepare for an exit he'd almost forgotten, or any other reason. What I'm saying is, that gap can close in a hurry, without notice, and you'll have neither a legal defense nor physical protection. Again, what an eternal price to pay for an attempt to save a little road time, or just for the thrill of being a little daring!

Bare head = blockhead

We've been through the helmet discussion in Chapter 4; but if anything belongs in a chapter dealing with recklessness, riding without a helmet does. What more can I say? Take a look at some cold, hard facts.

Chances are good your cycle was made in Japan. Cycles are a way of life there. Those smart people have seen fit to put crash helmet laws into effect, and since then their motorcycle deaths have been cut in half. Same story in Australia.

Closer to home, in a year when Idaho's helmet law was being contested and not enforced, deaths from head injuries rose to 75% of all motorcycle deaths. Then, states the Idaho Traffic Safety Commission, after the law was ruled constitutional and began to be enforced, those head-injury deaths dropped to 35% of the total.

A California study shows that almost *three times* as many head injuries occur among unhelmeted cyclists as when helmets are worn.

An engineering study made in Canada at the University of Ottawa involved 132 motorcycle accidents. In 53 of these cases, helmets were worn and impacted during the accidents. Of these, only 24 suffered head injuries, and only four were fatal. The other 20 sustained only minor concussions. I rest my case on this subject.

If you decide to ride smartly with head protection, bear in mind that most helmets are constructed well enough to take one tough blow and no more. If yours gets a good jolt when accidentally dropped, get a new one. It's the only safe thing to do.

Jerky motions

I suppose the one complaint I hear most often from motorists speaking their minds about cyclists is "they dart in and out of traffic like maniacs; it's almost impossible to keep from running over them!"

There is good reason for this negative reputation motorcycle operators as a class have with automobile drivers as a class. We have the reputation because too many cyclists *do* think the only way to ride is to dart in and out of traffic like maniacs. In a small town, a 16-year-old boy on a 100 cc bike was clipping along at 50 miles per hour in the right lane, with a big 18-wheeler just back of him headed the same direction in the left lane. The boy wanted to enter a private driveway a short distance ahead.

Instead of reducing his speed and dropping back behind the semi rig, he just jabbed the throttle to get all he could from about five horses in that 100 cc engine, and cut to the left right in front of that powerful tractor. Well, the trucker was going 55 miles per hour, which brought him unavoidably onto the bike. The poor guy left the scene rattled, for which he was later cited. Except for that, I'm positive he was helpless and innocent of the boy's death. It was just a chance no cyclist can afford to take. You can depend on it that cutting in front of vehicles will almost invariably have that result.

Actually, no matter how you place yourself in front of a more powerful vehicle, you're still going to be in big trouble. A 14-year-old kid on a 70 cc trail bike did a "wheelie" on it one day, right onto a state highway in front of an oncoming car—and without a helmet. One more senseless fatality statistic. One more motorist who will forever hate cyclists, and understandably so.

What you don't know——

That old saw about "what you don't know can't hurt you" is 180 degrees from the truth when it comes to riding a cycle. For instance, if you can't see what's ahead, it's a reckless act to pass another vehicle. If you'll check the law in your state, you'll probably find that passing on a hill or a curve is illegal as well as hazardous to the Nth degree. To these three taboos, add: passing at intersections or railroad crossings, on bridges, culverts or in tunnels of two-lane width, in "No Passing" zones, and anywhere you will have the sun in your eyes while passing.

Even riding too fast over a hill is a reckless act; you don't know what's on the other side, and you can easily find out too late.

Putting hazards "on hold"

One hazard at a time is more than enough to handle. That's why, when you're faced with two at once, you need to put one "on hold" if at all possible. For instance, if you're riding on a two-lane street in the business section, you might see a situation developing that would put you between one or more pedestrians on your right and an oncoming car on your left. Your solution is to move left in your lane and put more distance between you and unpredictable pedestrians, simultaneously reducing your speed to allow the car to pass the pedestrians before you do. Or you may speed up to pass them before coming abreast of the car, if that would serve better.

Suppose you are on a crosstown expressway and see a car at your right, getting ready to enter and merge into your lane. At the same time, you see a car in your rear-view mirror about to pass you on your left. To avoid the squeeze play, you can either speed up to pass the merging point before the entering car arrives—or slow down enough to let the passing car, the merging car or both complete their move without you in the middle. This decision will depend on relative speeds and distances separating the three vehicles, and the situation behind with respect to still other vehicles.

Let's say you are on a two-lane, one-way street and observe a motorist in the act of completing a parking maneuver ahead on your right. He will be getting out of his car about the time you pass him, and you need to move into the left lane to avoid this hazard. But your rear-view tells you there will also be a car in that left lane just when you need to use it. Again, you can move to the left side of the lane you're in, leaving the left lane for the car about to pass—and either reduce your speed or go a little faster to keep from being exactly alongside when the car door opens at your right. Or, depending on the speed of the car moving up in the left lane, you might speed up, give a very positive signal and move on into the left lane ahead of the car. This, however, calls for *very good* judgment as to the car's arrival time opposite the parked car. Generally speaking, it's hard to go wrong *reducing* your speed to provide separation between two hazards.

I could go on and on with more examples. Experience will be your teacher. The point I'm making is to use lateral maneuvering and speed changes to separate your hazards so that you will only have to deal with one at a time whenever this is possible.

Waiting in gear

How long does it take to press your toe against the gear pedal, to shift from neutral into first? A split-second. You need no "getaway" advantage sitting at an intersection, waiting for a green light, with first gear already engaged. When you glide up to an intersection stop, go into neutral and stay there until you need to go forward on the green.

I didn't fully appreciate why this is good advice until my clutch cable gave way in traffic one day. I managed to travel to my dealer's service shop with no clutch, because my particular bike could be shifted *without* the clutch through first, neutral and second gears. But each time I took off in low gear without the clutch action, it was a hairy, jerking experience. Now, if the cable had given way while I was waiting in first gear for a green light, the unexpected lurch forward could have meant a disastrous meeting with some of the cross traffic.

The same result would apply if for some reason your hand should slip off the clutch lever while you had your cycle in gear. One more good reason to wait in neutral: squeezing that clutch lever through long intersection waits is a good way to lower the service life of your clutch plates; and replacement isn't cheap.

Group riding risks

Some riders do fine traveling in groups, because they know how to do it properly, and resist the natural temptation to show off in front of friends. If you can't ride with some orderly discipline, you'll be better off riding alone. If you do any group riding, stagger your formation with the lead rider maintaining a left-of-center spot within his lane. Keep safe spacing between cyclists, increasing or decreasing these distances depending on group speed. *Don't bunch up* at intersections or anywhere else, until you park together at your destination.

If there is a slow-moving vehicle to be passed, go one at a time, and only when it is obviously safe. It should be understood that the leader will move ahead just enough to allow the others passing room, then return to the agreed-upon road speed. If a motorist breaks into the line of cyclists, the entire group should let him go on down the road and out of their hair as quickly as possible. Avoid blocking the highway; leave pull-in room for motorists between pairs of your group. Do *not* turn the occasion into a mass racing event.

When your group pulls off the road to eat or for rest stops, you have an opportunity to improve the image of the cyclist with the public—or help deteriorate it further than it is. We need all the good public relations we can get, on the road and off. On the road, we'll chalk up our best marks with the public when we're riding the safest.

A prime example of how *not* to ride with buddies is the case of two friends in my city—early 20's—one on a 450 cc and the other aboard a 750 cc. These guys thought they needed a routine something like the Ice Follies skaters as they purred along a four-lane city street at 35–40 miles per hour. As they approached various cars from behind, the rider on the right would pass on the right and the other would pass on the left. Then they would pull back alongside each other and ride on to the next conquest.

Obviously, one of the pair made an illegal pass each time, depending on which lane the car occupied. But that isn't what stopped their fun. What did it was a merging together after they passed their last car, that really *did* have them coming together. This time, they pulled too close and fast, collided and went out of control. One boy came out alive. He only skidded 26 feet on the paving on one side of his bike. The other wasn't so lucky. He traveled out of control 140 feet across the centerline into an oncoming pickup, and died at the scene. Legal, one-at-a-time passing would have avoided this tragedy.

Don't challenge Old Man Weather

I have ridden in rain, and I have ridden on snow when I was caught at work when it began to fall. No more. I will still ride in light rain if I am caught in an unexpected shower, but I really ride by the seat of my pants at slow speeds, knowing that early-rain surface is actually more slippery than it is after a good hour's downpour. If I have reason to believe it *might* rain, or when there is already a rain in progress, I do not take my cycle even a few blocks. I won't ride in fog at any time. And when winter really comes and the ice and snow season sets in, I put my bike up on the center stand under protective cover and leave it there until spring.

Cold, dry weather is O.K. in my book, *if* you can be comfortable and have no fogging problems with your visor or goggles. If your breath does condense on the inside of your helmet visor, rub a *light* coat of glycerine on it to prevent the fog-up. I wear warm wool socks in my boots, and tuck the tops under a pair of thermal drawers. Depending on the temperature, I may wear the thermal tops and/or a zippable quilted lining in my jacket. If it's *really* frigid outside, I'll wear a down-filled ski jacket my wife bought me, which also has the advantage of highly visible fluorescent color. My regular helmet keeps my ears warm.

You *can* have a problem with your brakes freezing up. If so, it just isn't worth it. If you try fighting the weather when the odds against your safety jump too much (such as when you tackle slick surfaces), you're just asking for trouble. And trouble seldom refuses, seldom needs coaxing, when you're on a motorcycle. To me, it's a heck of a lot more fun to confine my cycle riding to safe-weather periods and enjoy it season after season than it would be to try for year-round riding and not quite make it through all four seasons. There is plenty of excitement on those two wheels when the weather is good. *Don't challenge Old Man Weather.*

Riding when sleepy

I covered this in detail in Chapter 5; it's suicidal. And riding while you are emotionally upset, from depression to anger to grief, is just about as bad. You need all your faculties keenly honed to ride a motorcycle safely. And if you have a "don't care" attitude concerning your own safety, think about others out there in the streams of traffic who might become innocently involved.

Riding "high"

It's been said but it's worth repeating: your neck and that of anyone else around you will be on the block when you drink and ride, or when you try to combine two kinds of "trips" at once. It's suicidal and it's criminal. A 25-year-old man was cited for first-degree manslaughter in the death of a 24-year-old passenger on his 850 cc. The operator was drunk, and darting in and out of city traffic late at night. He hit a car, wrecked his cycle and the passenger was DOA. Civil lawsuits were added to his criminal charges. A very expensive and tragic drinking spree; and all so unnecessary.

Loose or bulky packages

I've seen large packages being carried loose, rested on the gas tank and the center area of the handlebars. Needless to say, manipulating hand controls was less than satisfactory, and negotiating corners almost impossible. Some things just aren't capable of being safely transported on a cycle. When you discover that's the kind of package you have, don't worry about "losing face" by deciding to leave it and use your car. It's better to lose face than to lose your life.

Even with luggage rack and tie-down cords, it is unsafe to carry objects that are too heavy, or to carry fluids in partially empty containers. (Every time you make a turn, the fluid weight shifts dangerously.) Do *not* use nylon rope in securing an object. Nylon too easily works loose with normal street bumps, and the rope can end up wrapped around your drive chain. From that moment, *anything* can happen to *you*.

A backpack is handy for carrying things, but don't try using one for an object that sticks up tall behind you. The wind can pull it out and cause you to wreck your cycle trying to grab for it. The safest use for a motorcyle is the original purpose: transportation for yourself.

Ignoring the law

I'll list this here because it is always a safety gamble. Traffic laws *exist* for the sake of safety and the orderly movement of vehicles. Both of these factors are more important to motorcycle operators than anyone else, because of their increased exposure to hazards.

This subject, however, is too vital to be treated in a few paragraphs. All of Chapter 9 has been devoted to the cyclist's relationship to traffic rules and regulations.

Dragging your feet

An important body protective precaution, easy to observe, is simply to keep your feet up on the pegs where they belong. Those few inches off the ground help a lot to avoid bruises or even broken bones from rocks or other obstructions occasionally encountered on the street. The fact that it *is* only occasionally that surface obstructions are encountered makes you just that much less alert to them—which makes it even more important to keep your feet on the pegs.

Hands on the grips!

One of the enjoyable things about cycling is the natural friendliness that prevails among most "Easy Riders." When I "lift a left" to salute a fellow cyclist, most respond readily. Some don't bother, but I like the practice.

One matter should be emphasized about this custom. *Don't* greet a fellow rider at the expense of safety for either of you. If you're at an intersection, both of you should have your hands full with clutch and throttle; it's no time to be waving "Hi!" You can still acknowledge the other with a horn tap, or a nod of the head.

The same greeting taboo is in effect when the streets are wet, or at a railroad crossing with both bikers angling across the tracks, or *any* circumstance requiring maximum concentration or both hands on the grips.

Switching fuel on the run

This isn't necessarily a distracting or dangerous operation for everyone. If your fuel valve is in a very convenient, easy-to-reach location and you practice enough, you should be able to switch from main to reserve while moving and never bobble. But if that isn't the case, make a practice of switching in advance of need. Otherwise, the moment you notice the telltale "running out" symptoms, pull over to make the change; or wait until you are temporarily halted at a traffic signal.

If you follow the "good to the last drop" practice, you can find yourself in a sputter-stall-nosedive antic. And if this happens to come as you pull away from a standing start into an intersection, with an impatient tailgater following, you can see what might happen next. Surprising nearby motorists doesn't make for happy endings.

Night riding

You'll find a full chapter discussion on this subject in Chapter 12. But I wanted to get it in this listing of reckless acts. The list would otherwise be incomplete.

Doubtless you will do some night riding. I do, too, when it's necessary and the distance is short. But it does constitute an extra riding risk at best. Avoid it if you can.

One of the Highway Patrol case histories of motorcycle fatalities uncovered in my research was a night riding case of the kind you *must* avoid to stay alive. A 20-year-old was riding down a graveled county road, left of the centerline. Perhaps we shouldn't consider this to be poor riding. He probably didn't know where the center of the road was. After all, it was gravel, and then, his cycle had *no lights!* You can see what a problem he had.

In this instance, a 22-year-old cyclist riding in the opposite direction down the same road got involved in the problem as well. When he belatedly caught sight of the first cycle, with no lights and headed directly for him, he took immediate evasive action. Hoping to avoid a head-on crash, Cyclist No. Two swerved to his left, into the lane Cyclist No. One should have been in. At the same time, unfortunately, Cyclist No. One decided to swerve right, for the same purpose. In the resulting impact, the second cycle was broadsided by the first. Cyclist No. One was killed; Cyclist No. Two sustained serious injuries.

So, in addition to the normal hazards of night riding, you could have them compounded by meeting another vehicle with no lights. They're tough to see until it's too late. I repeat, unless a night trip is really necessary, best do without it.

Riding too young

Another gambling hazard that belongs on this list even though it's covered in detail in the first chapter. "Too young" in my opinion is any age prior to 16. If you're not convinced, read Chapter 1 again and check with your Highway Patrol experts, and talk to some interns on duty at the hospital emergency wards in your city.

Nobody's business?

A country song that's been around for some time has the singer stating "it's nobody's business what I do." That's the attitude of a lot of cyclists who prefer the derring-do kind of riding and see nothing wrong with it.

The fallacy of this kind of thinking is that you automatically *make* it the business of others when you deliberately risk your neck in traffic. In upholding the Massachusetts compulsory helmet law for cyclists, the U.S. Supreme Court said among other things:

> "From the moment of injury, society picks the person up off the street or highway; delivers him to a municipal hospital and municipal doctors; provides him with unemployment compensation if, after recovery, he cannot replace his lost job; and, if the injury causes permanent disability, society may assume the responsibility for his and his family's sustenance. *We do not understand a state of mind that permits plaintiff to think that only he himself is concerned.*"

I think the court ruled properly. The argument that risk-taking by cyclists is nobody's business but their own just won't wash.

8. Speed Kills

UNLESS you are on a race track for the express purpose of risking life and limb for a $5 trophy cup or some very fleeting glory, speed for speed's sake should have no part of your motorcycle operation. Used as an economical and invigorating form of transportation, your cycle must always be controlled at safe, legal speeds.

The National Safety Council places excessive speed as the second most frequent traffic violation by cyclists. This is based on citations; other data indicate cycle riders may be in violation of speed laws even more often. For example, the "Maryland study" sponsored by the Motorcycle Safety Foundation looked at collisions between motorcycles and other vehicles. Where speed caused these collisions, in both urban and rural locations, the cyclist was the speeder in a staggering 97% of the cases!

One reason so many speeding cyclists have accidents is the effect it has on vision. Your field of vision—your ability to spot trouble before it happens—shrinks in direct ratio as your speed increases. Why make your life depend on your eyes, then hamper their effectiveness by too much speed?

Basic speed rule

Speeds that are legal are not always safe. The "Basic Speed Rule" as outlined in most Highway Patrol driver's manuals goes something like this:

"No vehicle shall be driven at a speed greater than is careful and prudent and not greater or less than is reasonable and proper, having due regard to the traffic, surface and width of the highway and of any other conditions then existing. And no person shall drive any vehicle upon a highway at a speed greater than will permit him to stop within the assured clear distance ahead."

Needless to say, this same basic rule applies to street travel when you are hauled in by the local police. It's a sensible rule that recognizes a simple truth. Suppose you are riding at a "legal" speed of 30 miles per hour on a city street when a ball bounces onto the street from behind a truck up ahead, parked alongside a playground. If you continue without slowing, and strike a child running to retrieve the ball, *you* will be cited for negligence. This set of circumstances makes slowing down a "reasonable and proper" thing to do. Why? Because the "assured clear distance ahead" became the far end of the truck, the moment the ball bounced from the playground onto the street ahead. You had no assurance that a child would *not* run from behind the truck. As a matter of fact, it became reasonable to assume this could happen suddenly. All of this became a part of the circumstances governing what would be a proper speed.

Speed-governing factors

Because of this basic rule of law, you are required, each time you ride and for the duration of your trip, to consider *everything* that might affect your safe operation, which also involves safety for others. Just a partial list of these factors to consider includes:

1. Number and speed of other vehicles on the roadway.

2. Presence of parked vehicles, pedestrians or cross-traffic.

3. Wide roadway or narrow?

4. Straight or curving?

5. Dry or wet?

6. Level or inclined?

7. Smooth or rough?

8. Are you approaching a truck crossing, construction site or accident scene?

9. Are you merging into or exiting from high-speed traffic?

10. Weather factors: rain, ice, snow, fog, wind, etc.

11. Presence of smoke, dust, sand, oil spots, etc.

12. Ability to see ahead under existing light conditions.

This last factor calls to mind the case of a 28-year-old aboard a 750 cc cycle. He was making an even 100 miles per hour *at night* when he hit a median curb and went airborne. You know what happened; may he rest in peace.

Posted limits

Within city boundaries, speed limits vary considerably. Sometimes as many as four different changes will be posted within a half-mile or so. *You* are responsible for keeping alert to these changes. The fact you failed to see a posted limit will never get you off without a fine, or worse if an accident is the result.

Speed and curves

Before the 55 miles-per-hour speed limit went into effect nationwide, 70 was legal on the interstate highways and certain expressways around cities. On one of these latter in my state, a 28-year-old was letting his 1,000 cc nuzzle that legal speed while he and his 26-year-old passenger approached a right curve. The "odor of alcohol" notation on the accident report may explain why the operator didn't reduce his speed for the curve; common sense certainly called for it. Both riders died when the big bike struck a guard rail, ejecting them with such force that the passenger tumbled 100 feet down the embankment.

Curves *cannot* be negotiated at the same speed you attain on straightaways. Reduce your speed before you begin to lean into the turn. Whether it is a curve, the sudden appearance of a ball in the street, an increase in the traffic flow, a rain shower, or any of a hundred different changes in your riding conditions, it is *your* responsibility to adjust for them—properly, and soon enough to proceed safely. You must keep in mind that a motorcycle is very vulnerable to *slick* surfaces and *rough* surfaces. *Be alert and adjust quickly.*

How fast can you stop?

You may not know just how far you would have to travel at various speeds before you could stop. Let's take a look:

Motorcycle Stopping Distances

	REACTION	BRAKING	TOTAL
20 mph:	20 Feet	20 Feet	40 Feet
30 mph:	30 "	45 "	75 Feet
40 mph:	40 "	80 "	120 Feet
50 mph:	50 "	125 "	175 Feet

NOTE: These distances will vary with size and weight of cycle, weight and ability of rider. (Reference: Motorcycle Safety Foundation.)

This chart is more recent than a similar one put out by the National Safety Council showing somewhat longer distances. Newer, better brakes may account for the difference. Variables entering into the picture according to both of these authorities include the type, size and weight of the motorcycle, the engineered ability of its braking system *and* the age and condition of the brakes, and the weight, experience and required reaction time of the operator. It wouldn't be a bad idea for you to enlist the help of a buddy to test *your* braking times at various speeds on *your* cycle. Be sure to use an off-street area for the test. If you show up better than the chart averages, be glad, don't be cocky. When your stops are for real, you might have an off day, or be so rattled your reaction time suffers.

Know your speed

It's wise to be a good judge of your speed, and that's something you can practice. The sure way to be aware of your speed, of course, is to glance often at your speedometer as you ride. That's what it's for, after all. Personally, I believe you *know* when you are going too fast for the traffic conditions surrounding you. Any time you *suspect* you may be traveling at an unsafe speed, slow down and live.

Speeding in pairs

Speeding alone is bad. Speeding while riding close alongside another cyclist is double trouble. Two men, one aboard a new 1,000 cc and the other riding a hot 900 cc, took a corner side-by-side at 65 miles per hour. Well, they *tried* to take it at 65 miles per hour. Their cycles collided in the intersection, and both men lost control. One died when his head struck a large boulder just off the street. The other lost his cycle but saved his life by jumping just before the 900 hit another boulder. Officially this was reported as a "following too close" accident; and surely that side-by-side cornering had a lot to do with the collision. But I can't help believing if they had been going 30 miles per hour instead of a crazy 65, there would have been a safer outcome.

Increase speed smoothly

When you do pull your throttle grip back for more speed, make it a smooth, gradual movement. Jerkiness does your engine no good, and can cause you to lose control of your machine. As you gear up, shift within the speed range your manual recommends.

Handling skids

Because skids are often associated with excessive speed in a braking or turning operation, let's consider some aspects of skidding. It's a hairy sensation, and you'll have to react quickly—hopefully as follows:

1. If your skid has been caused by over-braking, let up on them and try to keep your wheels rolling true.
2. If your skid is from too much speed, back off your throttle, still working to keep true contact with the riding surface.

3. If you must apply your brakes, do it *only* while your cycle is upright.

4. If your skid isn't too violent, you may be able to straighten up by using your feet. (Hopefully you have been smart enough to wear sturdy boots!) Trying to prevent a fall in a hard skid by using your feet is a last resort measure.

If this fails to sound reassuring about skid control, avoid skidding in the first place—*keep your speed sensible!*

Evasive speed

It doesn't happen too often, but there are a few occasions when *increasing* your speed is a bona fide safety measure. Generally this is when you are about to be hit by some motorist (the possibilities are numerous), and you want to evade. Please be sure you have a safe place to go in mind, as you speed up; and if a turning action is involved, be doubly careful.

Racing a passer

Speeding up to prevent another vehicle from passing you is rarely a legitimate safety move. Pull over and let him go. If he's dodging into a space between you and the vehicle ahead that will make the whole thing too close for comfort, drop back until there is only one tailgater traveling at a sharp clip.

Running from the police

Speeding to get away from the cops may sound exciting, but there's nothing smart or safe about it. Leave that for television. I knew a 20-year-old on a 750 cc who was sure he could shake the "fuzz." Before he struck a street sign, he pushed his bike up to 110 miles per hour! Actually he went out of control 156 feet before hitting the post, and stayed on for 190 more feet before he fell off. The cycle went another 32 feet beyond the point of death. There isn't a jail sentence in the world worse than that scene. As the slogan goes, *Speed kills!*

9. Obey the Law

MOTORCYCLE operators are required to observe the same set of rules in traffic that apply to motorists in automobiles. If you wait until you are 16 and have passed your driver's license exam, you will know what these rules are. If you are taking the under-16 risk, learn those rules and ride by them—they could save your life.

It's just as important for you to be prepared for the illegal maneuvers of others in traffic as it is to obey the rules yourself. Don't assume anything, much less that every motorist you meet will be diligent in observing the traffic regulations.

Observe posted signs

Part of observing the established traffic laws in your state and community will be to follow closely the directions given by posted traffic signs. Be alert to them as you ride the streets and roads. The number one priority among traffic signs will be to *observe the speed limit* at all times. The preceding chapter explains why this is vital to your safety, and common sense itself tells you why. But only you can exercise the maturity needed to ride within the speed limits regardless of the temptations to do otherwise.

Special cyclist laws

Your state and the various communities within it will also have laws on the books pertaining specifically to motorcycle operation. For example, if the state law fails to require you to travel with lights on at all times, but your community *does* require it, the local ordinance will apply. It's a case of "when in Rome, do as the Romans do." You will need to learn and observe both sets of laws, and not just to keep from "getting a ticket." Every law is designed for your safety by those who have learned from voluminous statistics what some of the key hazards for cyclists are.

A few of these rules for cyclists in my state of Oklahoma are required for younger riders only. Examples: you must wear an approved crash helmet if under 18; if under 16, you may not operate a cycle over 125 cc; you may not exceed 35 miles per hour; you may not carry passengers; and you may not ride legally between the hours of 9 P.M. and 4:30 A.M.

Regardless of age, no rider may carry passengers unless the cycle has a wheel diameter of at least twelve inches, and a double seat and double foot pegs. Cyclists may not hold onto any moving vehicle, may not ride on any sidewalk, and may not pass between lanes of traffic (riding the stripes). Every rider must have eye protection, with goggles (not sunglasses) or windshield fairing unless a visored helmet is worn. Some individual communities do require cyclists to ride with lights on day and night. Cycles under 125 cc are not permitted on our interstate highways (I'd hate to get on one with less than 500 cc!), and cycle owners must carry liability insurance.

Other state and local rules to check include any special licensing required, riding two abreast, parking laws, rules concerning equipment requirements (rear-view mirrors, safety bars, etc.), reflective materials required on cycle and/or rider, and whether there is a limit for handlebar height. All of this information can be obtained from your State Department of Public Safety and local police department.

Riding the stripes

As I mentioned in Chapter 7, riding the stripes between lanes of traffic headed your way is actually legal in California—though without right-of-way protection. But whether you live in California or any other state that may have decided not to give you a citation for the practice, there is a more important law against it: the law of self-preservation. Between-lanes is roadway roulette in its purest form.

Passing on the right

The same advice applies to that tempting practice of riding between parked cars and a moving line of traffic. Even if the traffic line is halted, it's both illegal and hazardous for you to ride your cycle between these cars and those parked at the curb. You never know when that inviting gap will be suddenly closed by the opening of a parked car door, or by the movement of a car in the line of traffic toward the parked cars. Observe the law by staying properly in the traffic flow, and avoid the risk.

One 16-year-old riding a 175 cc lost his life by passing a car on the right, next to the curb, and entering the intersection only to be struck by a car that was being maneuvered into an illegal left turn. It is worth restating that *impatience has no place on a motorcycle*. It is this same factor that has cost the lives of many cyclists who attempt to pass a car or truck in a no-passing zone. These zones are not there for the purpose of delaying your trip, but to save your life from hazards you can't see. Let them work for your safety—observe them!

Caution at the lights

Another easy-to-understand rule too often violated by both motorists and cyclists is observing signal lights properly. Stop when the light turns red and don't go until it has turned green again. Simple. Except, perhaps, for confusion about what to do when the light is amber. Some states make it legal to proceed on amber caution lights, at your own risk. Others make it clear the amber interval is for the express purpose of giving you time to come to a stop *before* the red. They don't want you mixing the two colors in the middle of the intersection, and will fine you for it. Of course, you never know which ruling has been learned by other vehicle operators. So the safe thing is *not* to proceed on amber.

Keep in mind that drivers of automobiles, with all of that solid steel protection, often push their luck at intersections. All too many will barrel across on a complete red signal, so long as they were close at the end of the caution light. The attitude is based on bluff. They know that very few people will tackle their speed and momentum with a slow and ineffective start-up pace. These red-light runners are growing in numbers all the time, and what it means for you is a *necessity* for a delayed startup at every intersection. Don't make a move until you are very sure what *all* the front-line drivers at the intersection are going to do. This may not seem very red-blooded, but it's much smarter than spilling yours.

Locally, a 16-year-old on a "C"-size cycle ran a red signal light at a high rate of speed. He laid down 97 feet of skid marks before colliding with a truck, but it wasn't enough to save his life. It just may be that this boy was going so fast he thought his best bet was not to risk a hard-braking skid, but ride right on through and take his chances. If so, excessive speed was his basic illegal error. You must realize there *is* a "point of no return" speed for a cyclist in traffic. Avoid it at all costs. "At all costs" is just an expression. But what *would* the cost have been to pursue a reasonable speed? A few minutes of the boy's time is all I can imagine. It would have been well worth sacrificing a *little* time rather than all of his life!

Signal your intent

"Motorcycle riders are required to signal all of their intentions just as a car driver is," says a Motorcycle Safety Foundation publication. You can do this with hand signals or light signals; but *do it*—for all turns, lane changes and stops. If motorists find it hard to see you anyway, they sure won't know you're making a turn or about to slow down unless you signal your intent.

I rely on my signal lights for all except special situations because I believe in keeping my hands on the grips where they belong. An example of the exceptions is a broad intersection where motorists have about seven different directional options. I am usually faced with opposing traffic at this intersection in such a way that these motorists are undecided about turning left in front of me. I appreciate this wholesome hesitance, but prefer them to go ahead and clear before I cross the intersection. To communicate this, I *briefly* remove my left hand and wave them forward. If I am in the midst of using my clutch, I give them a vigorous "Yes" nod of the head, and that is usually understood just as well.

Be sure to give your signals well in advance of your turn or stop. I find a quick squeeze-release action of the handbrake lever most helpful in warning traffic behind me of an impending stop.

Because so many of today's motorists see no earthly reason to signal their intentions to *you*, keep a very close watch. Learn the little movements, inclinations of the head or body, etc., that show a probability of turning. Give a sufficiently wide berth to others that you will have room to respond to emergencies that arise. Of course, when you are given the benefit of a signal, *pay attention to it.* Signaling a left turn in front of you may *not* mean the signaler will wait until you have passed by. It may mean "I'm turning left in front of you *now*, buddy!"

Tailgating

As I emphasize the illegality of this unsafe activity, let me say I do have a measure of repetition throughout this book. That's because many of the subjects covered apply to more than one discussion category, more than a single chapter. It also means that every such subject is serious enough to consider more than once—and the advice is worth memorizing.

Following too close is not only against the law, it's very dumb for a cyclist. The stopping distance chart in Chapter 8 gave 40 feet as an average at only 20 miles per hour. Just to make a point, let's say you're not average, you're super. You can react and stop in just 20 *feet* at that speed—the distance it takes most riders to simply *react.* Do you see where that would leave you in a sudden stop, if you're following as close as 15 feet? You really won't look good as a trunk-lid ornament, so *keep your distance*, Superman!

Excessive speed

You have just read an entire chapter on the subject of speeding and its consequences. The very least consequence will be paying fines, and if my city is typical, municipal ordinances are getting tougher and costlier on the speeder every year. We don't have a single moving violation any more that costs under $25. Check your own city. You may decide you can't even afford to speed from a pure *financial* standpoint. Speeding is against the law. You will get stopped more often on a cycle than you would speeding in a car; and it will be expensive. And, I repeat, that's the *least* consequence.

Riding left of center

Why would anybody riding a motorcycle want to ride left of center? That's a violation of the law, too. But even worse, it was the second highest cause of cycle accidents at non-intersection locations, according to the Maryland study reported by the Motorcycle Safety Foundation. Stay on your side of the road, and last longer. All it takes is paying attention to what you're about, and if you're not willing to do that much, stay off of motorcycles.

Failure to yield

Failure to yield the right-of-way to another vehicle is a prime cause of accidents, and a violation that pays off big down at police headquarters. It happens to be the number one cause of cycle accidents in my state, and a fourth of the time it is the motorcycle operator who is at fault. Believe me, there should be *no* occasions when a cyclist fails to yield to another vehicle. The odds are all in favor of the other guy when it comes to surviving in one piece. It's also a quick way to lose insurance coverage, or have your premiums raised out of sight. Play it cool and give the people what the law says they're entitled to have.

And don't forget that 75% figure. That's how often the *other guy* will fail to give *you* the right-of-way. And no matter how righteous that makes you feel, it won't replace even a broken leg. What it comes down to is this: *Give up* the right-of-way, no matter *who* the law says is entitled to it. Chapter 14 discusses this matter thoroughly.

Median crossing

Ever cross a median at a non-crossing point? I tried once, even though it's against the law. I didn't quite make it; and what happened inspired this whole chapter. It was the worst accident of my riding career to date. If I have one to top it, I won't live to write about it. Ignoring the rules on that occasion would have ended my riding career if it had been something bigger than the VW that sent me sprawling across 20 feet of interstate highway.

I almost convinced myself I was just an innocent victim of circumstances in this situation, because of all the *right* things I did, and all the *wrong* things done by the VW driver. I had just exited from one interstate onto the north two lanes of another, headed west. I checked both rear-view mirrors and saw that all was clear behind me from the east. Then I switched on my amber left-turn signals (my oversize red tail light was already shining brightly) and began moving left to the inside lane. So far, so good. Much better than the VW driver, who came abruptly onto the scene over the crest of a fairly steep downgrade sloping in my direction. He was, in my experienced judgment, making a good 70 miles per hour—he admitted to "more than 60" when the state trooper questioned him. He was groggy and low on reflexes after being on the road with only brief rest stops for about 34 hours. His only move was to honk like mad until he hit me a glancing but effective blow; no brake action until the impact.

Now if that's all there was that led to the accident (which sent my cycle and me on that crazy ride diagonally back across the highway just as more traffic topped the rise), I could have gone on feeling guiltless. I thought the trooper gave the citation to the wrong guy, and I paid a fine under protest. (Though my bike was badly damaged, I stayed with it until the end, got up quickly and helped stop oncoming traffic and drag the cycle off onto the median.)

But that isn't all there was. What I had to admit to the VW driver and the trooper was what earned me the citation. I had intended to *cross* the median at this point, where I noted a well-worn grassless area indicating that many others had done just that. And while I never actually crossed the median at an unauthorized point, I *was* in the process of trying. You might still think I got a raw deal, until I tell you it was only possible to view oncoming westbound traffic for about a 550-foot span up the hill from my collision point. And because the median crossing would have been illegal at this point, any oncoming driver could logically say, "I couldn't see any reason for him to be moving across my lane. I didn't believe it. He had nowhere to go!" And in substance, that's what the VW driver said.

So what I did by my illegal maneuver was to confuse an oncoming driver, even though he himself was exceeding the legal speed limit. Had I stayed in my original lane until I reached the official median crossing farther west, I would have found time to make the lane change safely. And that's why I was cited—for changing lanes *unsafely*. It was unsafe because it *could* confuse an oncoming driver in the absence of an authorized median crossing there. The lesson I learned and am trying to communicate is: to stay alive, *obey the law!*

Shoulder riding

Riding on shoulders is also illegal, and for good reason. Usually they are of a loose, soft surface that can upset a cyclist easily—or apt to have "quick-spill" materials scattered upon them even when the surface of the shoulder is paved. They are not motorcycle paths; they are emergency stopping zones. If you try saving a little time by passing a long line of motorists on the right, using the shoulder area, you can't know when one *will* pull off for an emergency stop. You even risk running afoul of a motorist as impatient as you in that long line, who suddenly decides to make the same illegal use of the shoulder, right in your face. Bear in mind you are subject to the same traffic rules those motorists are and, among other things, this means *don't* try to turn shoulders into private freeways.

Face the citation!

Trying to run from the police is certainly illegal everywhere. As was seen in the preceding chapter, it can also prove fatal when you're fleeing on a motorcycle. Another case involved a 46-year-old man who was riding a minibike at night without lights, on a lakefront road. He had been drinking, and failed to stop for a patrol car with its light and siren going. He ran into a pair of closed park gates, and later died of head injuries.

I had planned to cite just this one "running-from-the-law" example here and go on. But even as I worked on this chapter, another tragic example of this particular folly made local headlines. I have decided to include it as well, putting *you* right on the cycle—because I have no way of knowing how you will think and react at some future time if you find yourself in a similar situation. Here it is, recreated out of today's newspaper account.

You are 18. You've been riding a hot cycle quite awhile, and know how to handle it well. You know it will leave most cars behind at an intersection as if they were turtles. The speedometer hints it should double the maximum legal highway speed. You've picked up your 17-year-old pal, and he's hanging on behind you as you slip easily through the night traffic. You're bareheaded, because it seemed only fair to let your friend have your skid-lid; after all, you have the controls.

Here's an intersection up ahead, with an amber signal light just coming on. You probably could have stopped, but it just seemed a little more exciting to push on through as the light changed to red, and roar off in a power gear. Oops! As your buddy leans a little, you catch a glimpse of a patrol car in your rear-view, and you wonder if he saw you run the light. He's moving in behind you now.

Another intersection; you're being very law-abiding now, but still wonder if the cop is just watching to see what you'll do next. After the light turns green, you only get 100 yards past this intersection before you have your answer. The red blinker light atop the patrol car comes on. He wants you to pull over and take the rap. You have other ideas. You shift your bomb down and tell your friend to hang on tight, then off you go, at speeds that finally exceed 90 miles per hour. But still that persistent cop is on your tail. You thread your bike between two lanes of cars waiting for a light to change, thinking you can lose the cruiser, but those motorists just move apart and let him come on through.

What to do? The guy must have a souped-up power plant, and it's obviously going to take something more daring to shake him. (Sure, you could have slowed down and let him take you downtown, but the charges are compounding now, and it just didn't seem like the thing to do at the time.) So you make a *big* move, veering suddenly across the median to change from your westbound expressway lane to the *eastbound* ribbon. *Nobody* would follow you into *this*. But he does; and, as that eastbound traffic shucks off both sides of the expressway to let your cycle and his patrol car pass in the wrong direction at those scary high speeds, he even seems to be gaining a little.

Luckily you haven't hit anyone yet—but,—here's a Jeep Bronco that doesn't look like it will get out of the way! Swerve again! You've *got* to miss him. . . !

The bike operator made his last mistake by swerving the wrong way. He took the same direction the Bronco driver chose, at the same time. The head-on impact, even with the eastbound driver braking for all he was worth, carried the motorcycle 26 feet backward, killing one cyclist instantly. The other was dead on arrival.

Like I say, I don't know who you are, or how you will react if you ever find yourself in a similar situation. I'd like very much to think you will recall reading about this tragedy, and decide quickly it's *not* for you. No traffic violation arrest you'll ever face is so bad it's worth risking your life to avoid. So, if you have disobeyed *one* law, face it, learn your lesson and live to *obey the law* tomorrow!

10. Riding Double

USUALLY, state laws require a motorcycle to be equipped with passenger seating, passenger foot pegs, and wheels 12 inches or more in diameter before passenger carrying is legal. The operator must be 16 or older. Some states also require the wearing of helmets, by both riders. Riding sidesaddle is illegal in all but a few states, and thoroughly dangerous anywhere. Check out the law in your state before even considering carrying passengers or riding as a passenger with some other operator.

What safety dictates

The Motorcycle Safety Foundation says you can never carry more than one passenger, and that as a beginning rider you shouldn't carry any at all. It also advises that you instruct your passenger on how to ride, and be responsible for their safe clothing and helmet protection. I'll go even further and say that maximum safety dictates that you just forget about carrying passengers, or *being* one.

Passenger carrying can make your cycle a completely unfamiliar machine. It alters your balance, control and weight factors *and* it increases your chances of accidents. I'm against *anything* that does that. However, I know it is very tempting to ride double. I'm happy my wife decided to give up riding with me after we took a couple of road trips on my lightweight (200 cc) commuter bike.

Our first jaunt was only 30 miles into the country, but we chose a winter day when the temperature was anything but comfortable. By the time our round-trip was over, it took an hour to thaw out. The second occasion was in good weather, but the distance was too ambitious for my cycle. My wife sat behind me holding on for dear life over a state highway trip of 160 miles. The wind blast, inability to see where we were heading, and merciless vibration (she only weighs 110, and I hadn't altered the suspension) convinced her that kind of thing just wasn't a joy.

Changes you can expect

If you do take a passenger along, here are some important changes from the normal handling conditions with your cycle:

1. Tire pressures and shock absorber settings will need to be adjusted to compensate for the extra weight aboard. Consult your manual or dealer. By all means, *don't* add a passenger's weight to questionable tires. A Safety Research Center study by the University of North Carolina indicated the presence of passengers in 60% of the accidents involving blowouts.

2. You will have less seat room, and are either moved forward into an unfamiliar and possibly uncomfortable position with regard to controls, or your passenger will suffer on the rear edge of the seat. You will also be shifting the weight distribution too far back for good operation.

3. With the added weight, the center of gravity is also changed, and the bike handles differently. The difference may not be radical, but in an emergency it may *seem* radical. Stops are more difficult, and your upshifting takeoffs are no longer smooth.

4. Taking turns and corners that seem easy riding alone can be a struggle with a passenger aboard who tends to counteract your inside lean with an opposite lean.

5. Going up or down a steep hill is entirely different with two aboard. You now have too much weight on the low (rear) side as you climb, and, going steeply downhill, your passenger's weight can force you into awkward controls handling or bad steering.

6. The distraction factor is multiplied, by more than two. Your concentration is automatically lowered, and you can easily find yourself talking or "being cute" at a time when you need to be *extra* alert and drive with *extra* caution.

Things that help

So much for the problems of riding double. Are there any helpful things to do? Here are some:

1. Make sure your cycle is "built for two," with a proper seat and foot pegs for an additional rider. Invest in a "sissy bar" and an extra helmet with visor or goggles. The backrest will give your passenger extra comfort, and the helmet and visor will provide necessary protection.

2. Passengers also have the same needs you do for boots and protective clothing. Your passenger must *not* wear a loose scarf, or anything like floppy pant legs or long shoelaces that might get caught in the drive chain or spokes.

3. If you will be riding more than a few miles, adjust your shocks and tire pressure to compensate for the extra weight. If your passenger is more than 150 pounds in weight, check

with your dealer about the hazard of overloading your size and model of motorcycle. If he advises against it, heed the advice or be prepared for a civil lawsuit should you survive an accident in which your passenger is killed or injured. (This can happen regardless of your precautions; but the measures you take will influence the outcome.)

4. Instruct your passenger to use the "grab bar" (passenger handhold) or to hold securely onto your waist (*not* your jacket). Caution him or her to coordinate any leaning with your own, and to sit without fidgeting or twisting around to see what is happening behind. Also make a strong point about keeping both feet on the pegs, even at intersection stops. A fast takeoff can *unseat* a "feet-down" passenger.

5. For your part, start up your engine and have both feet firmly on the ground for balance before allowing your passenger to mount. Then accelerate more deliberately, ride at slower speeds than you normally do, stay farther behind vehicles ahead, take all curves and corners more cautiously, and come to longer, more gentle stops.

O.K. I've told you more than I really want to about *how* to ride double. The best thing is simply not to court double trouble at all. Motorcycle riding is basically intended as a one-person form of transportation, and it's definitely safer to keep it that way. When you realize that only about 10% of the nation's motorcycle operators carry passengers on the majority of their trips, it becomes pretty revealing to note that they account for 17% of the accidents! It's just much more dangerous sitting on the uncomfortable rear inches of a saddle, holding onto a waist or grab bar, than it is to sit in the "driver's seat" with your hands and feet on the controls.

I would never ride as a passenger on a motorcycle with anyone. The passenger has no control, and must put his life entirely in the hands of the cycle operator, who may or may *not* be that trustworthy. When a 24-year-old girl took a ride around a local lake with her 28-year-old boyfriend, she probably didn't think it would be her death ride. Even though he *had* been drinking. He owned a 900 cc, and showed it off at an unsafe speed. They went off the lake road that crosses the dam, struck a guard rail after 13 feet, slid on the cycle's side another 15 feet, hit a guard rail post, went another 13 feet and struck another post, and wound up 29 feet farther on, back on the roadway. Both were killed.

More risks are taken

Riding double involves one hazard few people may think about, but which is nonetheless real. Again, this applies primarily (though not exclusively) to younger riders. The records in motorcycle fatality cases reveal a definite tendency on the part of operators aged 25 and under to take more deliberate risks when there is a passenger hanging on behind. I'm not a psychologist, so I asked a good one why this would be the case.

Dr. Ronald G. Seaborn, Ph.D. and Clinical Psychologist in Oklahoma City, confirmed the validity of the statistical findings from a psychological standpoint.

"When a person is alone," he said, "he feels more insecure—less confident of being able to handle whatever situation might be coming up as he rides his motorcycle. It's like the child who doesn't have enough nerve to go into the woods alone, but with another person, he feels more secure and ventures in. The cyclist riding alone is more cautious because of this same basic insecurity. With another person, even a passenger who can't assist with the controls, his own sense of security causes him to ride with more boldness; and this translates into even greater risk-taking."

I hadn't even thought of that possibility. I was simply of the opinion that the operator would be apt to "show off" before a passenger. Dr. Seaborn readily agreed, saying "that happens without a doubt, even with those who are excellent motorcycle riders from the standpoint of pure mechanical operating proficiency."

The trend was very obvious in the fatality records I studied at the Oklahoma Department of Public Safety. Of 20 fatal accidents over a 2-1/2-year period, all involving cycle operators 25 years of age and under and carrying passengers at the time of the accident, *only one* accident (a tire blowout) could be said to result *without* deliberate risk on the part of the operator. Even this could have been influenced by the extra weight being carried. If the operator knew of his bad tires and added passenger weight in spite of it, that's a deliberate risk in my book. I believe all the risks involved in riding double are too plain to ignore.

If you are a 25-or-under cyclist, resist the temptation to carry passengers, for the safety of *both* of you. If you are invited by such a cyclist to hop on for a spin, have the guts to say thanks but no thanks. Remember, you won't have one iota of control over what happens; and you will be going into what is probably the riskiest single undertaking in cycling today, with your eyes wide open. In those 20 cases mentioned before, there were 31 deaths—15 of them *passengers!*

11. Intersection Alertness

THERE SEEMS to be little doubt that the intersection is your nastiest nemesis from the standpoint of the most accident-prone location. Accidents can and do happen midblock and on low-traffic county roads. But statistics nationwide, statewide and locally indicate that *more* accidents occur at intersections. It's logical. There you have vehicles approaching you from several directions at once. You and motorists alike are busy watching traffic signals, other vehicles, pedestrians, advertising signs and pretty girls—while slowing, stopping, starting, accelerating and changing gears. Chances for unwanted involvement just naturally increase at intersections, so they just as naturally call for greater caution.

The National Safety Council reports on a New York study of collisions between motorcycles and other vehicles. Almost exactly two-thirds of the accidents studied were in right-angle collisions at intersections, driveways and parking lot entrances.

A broader study made by the Motorcycle Safety Foundation put the figure lower, but this was still the highest danger point of all locations. Seventy-two per cent of these accidents had the motorcycle striking the other vehicle and, regardless of which vehicle was struck, it took the impact on the *left side* three-fourths of the time. The *cause* of 90% of these collisions was simple: Failure to yield the right-of-way! I'll have more to say about this in Chapter 14.

One of the most typical motorcycle fatalities, perhaps the single most typical, took the life of a 34-year-old rider. On his 750 cc machine, he was doing everything he was supposed to according to the traffic laws. But a motorist failed to yield him his right-of-way at an intersection, and he was killed. By *survival* standards, the cyclist was at fault!

If you disagree with my conclusion, you're not yet ready to ride a motorcycle safely. It is the motorist who is most often guilty of failing to yield the right-of-way at intersections, but it is the *cyclist* who gets *killed*. If you insist on your legal rights at the expense of your own safety in an intersection encounter, *you* are at fault. It's as simple and as deadly as that.

Many different types

An intersection gets its name from the fact that traffic from different directions intersects there. This is the principal reason for its extra hazard to you; other vehicles can cross your path from at least two other directions, and sometimes from *four* other lanes. Keeping an eagle eye on all this traffic plus overtakers in your own lane can be quite a chore, but it's necessary. Motorists at cross-traffic stop signs often become impatient and move ahead "out of turn."

Not all intersections are alike by any means. Some are nice and open, with good visibility in all directions. Others will almost give you claustrophobia, with tall buildings crowding the sidewalks at all four corners. Some will regulate traffic by an array of signal lights; others will have four-way stop signs. Some will control only two directions by stop or yield signs, and still others will be completely open, with only the standard rule requiring drivers to yield to a vehicle on the right arriving at the intersection at the same time. Speed limits will vary at different intersections. Some intersections will simply be where driveways join with a street. Some will involve railway tracks and barriers that lower across the roadway. Some will be well-marked with signs indicating the nature of the intersection, and what you can and can't do legally, and these rules can vary by season and by hours of the day. Others not only give you no warning of intersecting drives, etc., but conceal them from your view with shrubbery.

Safety alert measures

All of this calls for special alertness as you approach any kind of intersection. You need to be aware of the traffic behind you before you arrive, leaving you visual scanning time for an inspection of every opposing lane (ahead, or at either side). If a stop is called for, make it a *complete* stop, not just a hesitation. Be aware of the speed of every vehicle you might come near as you approach, move into and through the intersection. If you see an overtaker in your rear-view that appears to have too much speed, or even no intention to stop, prepare to take necessary defensive measures. Use your peripheral vision, but also keep your head moving from side to side, to give you a complete panoramic picture of all vehicle activity.

Be alert at the lights

If the light is green as you approach the intersection, and remains green, look over all opposing traffic and decide whether they are going to honor your right-of-way. If so, proceed briskly across, always alert to the possibility someone could change his mind. You must remember you are invisible to some motorists, and if one of them "jumps the gun" as the light begins to change from GO to CAUTION for your lane, you could be run down. Be ready for a motorist coming across from the opposite direction to cut left in front of you without signaling—*the deadliest move in traffic today for cyclists.* Sometimes you can tell by the set of his head, or his reduced speed, that he has a left turn in mind. But too many fail to signal; and it's safer to *expect* a turn and be wrong than to expect him to drive *straight* through and be wrong.

A 56-year-old man on one of the first GL-1000 machines sold in my state fell victim to a pickup driver at an intersection. It was 6 P.M. and light enough for good visibility, but the pickup driver, who had been drinking, claimed he "didn't see" the cyclist as he turned left directly into the big bike's path. After the impact, the cycle was spun into a two-ton truck in the cross-traffic.

If you have approached the intersection properly alert, you will have a good idea as to whether the green you enter upon has just started, or is about to change. If the latter is true, slow down and be extra cautious. It is better to start coming to a halt a little early than to enter the intersection just as the green changes to amber. Of course, you will need to know whether another vehicle is crowding your tail light—and if possible, whether this driver seems impatient—before you shut down, even on a full amber caution light.

If the caution light is on before you arrive at the intersection, slow down with positive action and stop. Part of the "positive action" may be warning a motorist behind your cycle that you are stopping—and this can be done by turning half around and giving him a hand indication, or by tapping your tail light in a warning series of flashes, using the hand brake lever gently. You must make an exception to this procedure if the local law or custom in your community calls for crossing the intersection on the amber caution light. But be very alert when you do this; you could be run down by some cross-traffic motorist from a community like mine, where amber means *come to a stop*.

One good way to avoid problems of this nature is to look ahead as you ride toward a signal-light intersection, and control your speed such that you arrive at the entering point shortly after the signal has given your lane the green light. I try to do this, and on familiar routes I seldom have to touch foot to pavement. If you do have to stop at a signal intersection, do it just as you would in a car—don't try to squeeze in between lanes. Don't dart in and out or make unnecessary lane changes as you approach, just to show off the superior mobility of the cycle. I have already recommended you shift into neutral as you come to an intersection stop. Let me add that if your approach is on a rough or "washboard" surface, you need to delay part of this shifting operation *until* you stop. You need a firm grip with both hands on such a surface.

Be cautious about the car in front of you when the GO signal comes on. It can be very embarrassing to start confidently up at the same speed as the car ahead, with very little space separating you, only to have the driver of that car suddenly stop. You may think this is highly unlikely, but it happened to me. The car ahead was in a left-turn lane, and I was right behind. As the lady driver started up, she saw a motorist across the intersection start up too early on a straight-ahead course. Fearing a collision, she stomped on her brakes; and, because I had neither expected this nor left sufficient space between us, I ran into her. This was during my early riding days, and it was a lesson well learned. I now make sure everything is going all right ahead before starting up; and I proceed ahead with the same caution, with good separation space.

The car ahead of you *could* stop unexpectedly for various mechanical reasons, or, because the driver has seen a hat blow into his path, or a small dog dart in front of him, something you didn't see. Whatever the reason, it can happen, and you need to expect the unexpected.

Beware timing changes

Familiar routes are best to travel, but there is one danger. If the signal-light timing sequence on your route hasn't varied for months, that is no guarantee they'll be the same tomorrow. If you're accustomed to having one of a series of traffic lights turn green just before you hit the intersection, you may unconsciously be pushing the red a bit close. You may even feel a little cocky about your "insider's knowledge" that enables you to move through that intersection without interrupting your smooth pace, knowing from experience that the light will turn green exactly when you move into the intersection, making you both legal and early in crossing.

As I say, you have no guarantee whatever. Tomorrow could be the day when the lights have been changed in timing. If you start merrily through at normal throttle, expecting to have a GO signal when you enter the intersection, you may have to stand on your head to keep from being hit by cross-traffic. The rule to observe is simple. *Don't* proceed into an intersection unless you *have* the green light. Ride by what your eyes see, not what your memory tells you has been true for many months. Otherwise you could die of assumption.

Oncoming vehicles hazard

Keep in mind that your greatest danger is from any vehicle in a position to collide with you from the left side. But as a practical matter, I consider any vehicle approaching me from any direction to be a threat. If a motorist is coming toward you from the opposite direction, and a shopping complex driveway is at your right, *assume* he will turn left in front of you to enter that driveway. Do this even in the absence of any signal on his part, because of the growing habit of failing to signal, along with failing to yield the right-of-way. If such a motorist doesn't turn in front of you, be grateful. If he did while you *weren't* anticipating the possibility, it could be disastrous.

If you have intersection traffic to your right or left, don't make a move into the intersection until you are sure what their intentions are, and then be ready to dodge. If you have taken my advice and installed air horns, you can use them if opposing intersection traffic threatens your right-of-way privileges. You can *use* them—but *never rely* on them.

Lane center hazard

Try not to stop at an intersection in line with the gasoline filler spout of a vehicle immediately ahead. Normally, this means center-of-lane position. One of the few times I have gone down on a street was caused by such a stopping position. The car ahead had just driven away from a service station, where the gas tank cap had not been replaced. On starting up, gasoline sloshed out of the tank onto the center crown of greasy gunk accumulated over the months—just as I was getting underway. Immediately, the surface under my front tire was so slippery that my cycle went down before I knew what was happening.

Sure, that sort of thing is rare. It may never happen to me again.

But I was just lucky that no motorist was right behind me on that occasion, or that sparks from my slipping cycle didn't ignite the spilled gasoline. So my advice is: *Don't stop behind filler spouts* at intersections. Most often, that means avoid the center-of-the-lane position. Pickup trucks, etc., with filler spouts at the side, will be the exceptions to this rule.

Vision hazards

When anything blocks your view of traffic at an intersection (buildings, plantings, parked cars or trucks, etc.), make your approach in such a way that you don't get an unwelcome surprise. The best defense is to reduce your speed and increase your alertness. *Ease* forward until you can see what you are headed into, and what might be headed for you.

Residential intersections are generally more "closed in," with more trees, shrubs, etc. to block your view of the streets you are crossing. *Do not* rely on yield signs or even stop signs to protect you from motorists in residential areas. Having the legal right-of-way is small consolation for broken bones or worse. I have had a camper pickup come right through a yield sign on my left as I entered the intersection, forcing me all the way to the right before the driver finally came to a stop. He was scared and apologetic. He had been looking directly at me, yet had never seen me! In his defense, he *was* driving toward an early morning sun—just one more very real hazard at an intersection.

Don't be invisible

This prompts me to caution you to *make yourself visible* to other vehicle operators, or do all you can to that end. If you stop behind a car at an intersection, don't occupy a "blind spot" with relation to his rear-view mirror. When there is a *working* outside mirror (not a floppy, unused one), line up behind it. Otherwise, be sure you are visible from the center-mounted inside rear-view. You are usually visible from both of these if your cycle is in line with the auto's left wheels.

Four-count eye scan

In residential areas, I consciously and deliberately give *four full sweeps for vision* at each intersection. I turn my head left, then right, then left and right again, as I approach and enter. Once left and once right won't do it. Of course, zipping right on through an intersection with never a glance to either side (as I see some cyclists ride) is sheer suicide. Give it *all four counts*, and really swivel your head so you can see everything that's going on in both directions down that street you are crossing. The closer you get to the intersection, the faster your eye-sweep, until it feels as though you are shaking your head to say "No." If that sounds foolish, just remember it's life insurance!

Home driveway hazard

Residential driveways are sometimes nightmares, with neither you nor the driver backing out into the street able to see one another. It will be your responsibility to hold yourself ready for such emergencies, with brakes "at ready" and speed at a minimum until the potential hazard is passed. When you see a car backing out as described, let him see or hear you before you reach his driveway. Those air horns are handy at times like this.

Passing rule

Do you know what your state law says about passing near an intersection? In mine, it is illegal to pass another vehicle within 100 feet of any intersection including a railroad crossing. A 17-year-old girl would not have died here in my city if the 21-year-old operator of an 850 cc cycle had observed this law. She was a passenger on his bike when he passed a car at the precise moment that motorist made a left turn into a side street. The cyclist was speeding, and may have thought he could complete his passing before the car could move left. He may have made his move because he saw no left-turn signal. At any rate, he was injured and his girlfriend was killed because of his illegal, unsafe actions at the intersection. *Never move to pass a vehicle within 100 feet of any intersection!*

Foot traffic hazard

One more hazard of the intersection is people crossing the street. If there is a signal light, pedestrians generally heed it, but not always. One thing you can depend on: if you injure a pedestrian, even one who has risked jaywalking in the middle of the block, you are the one who will "get it in the neck." Pedestrians almost invariably have the right-of-way. I won't buck them even when I have a full green light.

When pedestrians are present at an intersection, make your stop with feet down before proceeding—and be especially alert as you start up again. Watch closely, particularly when you are making a right turn, a situation that can easily bring you into quick successive contact with two streams of pedestrians at right angles to each other.

12. Riding at Night

FOR MAXIMUM safety, you would have to forget about night riding, because you just can't *see* well enough. But I know there will be some who must ride at night, at least part of the time. I'm included in that category, because of a telephone message taping for my church that must be done at or near midnight each Sunday. The round trip is just under three miles. So, I take my clear-visored helmet and go. If this route were not so well-lighted by the city's arc-type street lights every block of the way, I would fire up my compact instead. One thing I *won't* do, even for three miles, is ride my cycle at night when it's raining or otherwise slick. If this is the condition Sunday midnight, I take the car.

Two plus factors

You can say there are two *positive* factors on the side of night riding. Generally speaking, traffic is lighter, *and* you can usually see approaching headlights for a good distance. But those are the only plus factors I can think of offhand. (And about those headlights from other vehicles, I have known cases of some that for one reason or another have driven *without* lights, which doesn't help a night riding cyclist one whit.)

Many negative factors

Colliding with another vehicle isn't your only concern in riding at night. The Maryland study quoted previously established that single-vehicle motorcycle accidents occur more frequently in darkness, by a significant figure. A 31-year-old riding a 400 cc cycle was killed at night. His single-vehicle accident resulted from going into a curve too fast and failing to make it. The curve was a left upgrade; the asphalt paving was dry. He ran off the roadway onto a dirt shoulder and after traveling 310 feet, struck some granite blocks. The rider was thrown from the cycle back into the center of the roadway and killed instantly. Daylight vision could easily have made the difference by identifying his hazard so well that he might have reduced his speed the necessary amount to successfully negotiate the curve. Speeding and darkness make a deadly combination.

Easy to override

Your speed should always be reduced for night riding, because you simply cannot see as well or as far as you can during the day. Overriding your headlights is bad with any vehicle, and it's very easy to do on a cycle. I have already stressed the fact that every time you ride, *you bet your life on your eyes.* Hills and curves become greater riding hazards at night, and you will be slower to recognize dangerous conditions of the roadway itself, or to see objects on the street or highway that pose a threat to you.

One 30-year-old was riding a 750 cc about 55 miles per hour on a state highway at night, with no helmet. He struck a horse that ran onto the highway, and both bike and rider flew about 50 feet through the air before the rider was ejected. The cycle went another 189 feet; the rider died of head injuries. In daylight, seeing the horse in time could have made the difference in this case.

There is no question that a 35-year-old riding a 350 cc bike could have averted his death if he had been out during daylight hours. He was also making about 55 miles per hour on a county road at night, when he hit a stalled truck that was without lights. This cyclist was overriding his headlight to such an extent that the stalled truck took him by complete surprise; no skid marks were laid down before the fatal impact.

Animals of dark color, pedestrians wearing dark clothing, unlighted vehicles, and the like all present far greater hazards at night. Both the time required for identification and reaction time are longer at night. If an oncoming vehicle shows only one headlight, don't assume it's a fellow cyclist. Ride to the right, so that you don't risk tangling with the dark left headlight of a "one-eyed" car. One other hazard is greater at night: "the drunks are out" in greater numbers. Your chances of running into trouble with careless driving on the part of other vehicle operators increase from this standpoint.

Complete darkness isn't the only extra-danger time. The late afternoon hours merging into dusk have always proved to be high-accident hours. Sharpen your reflexes during this period.

Care and use of lights

Night riding requires your lights to be in good working order, and *clean*. *Caution:* Due to bulb or wiring problems, you can have a good, strong brake light with no tail light at all. Inspect all lights before any night trip, for any deficiency. To prevent burning out the low-beam capacity in your headlight too soon, try to equalize the time each beam is used. At night, use the high beam except when meeting or following another vehicle. Then be prepared to give the same courtesy as to "dimming" that you would if you were driving a car. Use your low-beam for daylight riding.

Switching off of your high beam is a matter of safety as well as courtesy. Even though you have only one headlight, it can be just as bothersome to oncoming drivers as the brights on another automobile. As you go to low beam, remember to reduce your speed accordingly. If an oncoming motorist fails to dim his lights, the glare can be hazardous to you in its severity. It will help some to focus your eyes to the right side of the roadway ahead. Your peripheral vision will keep tabs on the car as it passes.

Let's hope you never experience fog while riding your cycle at night. But if you do, or if bad weather has impaired visibility, use your *low beam.* Refraction causes the high beam to reflect back into your own eyes, almost as it would to point your headlight into a mirror.

Beam setting

Don't take it for granted that the headlight is set properly for you when you buy your cycle. It's easy to raise or lower, and worth the bother. Usually, just a very slight change will do the trick. Check it out at night to make sure it's right for your riding habits and vision. Recheck the setting periodically. The adjustment can be affected by no more than riding over rough surfaces. Your bright beam should give you adequate visibility for a good city block. If it doesn't, ask your dealer to check out your headlight problem before you get into trouble.

If your headlight should go out at night, try switching to the other beam. Then pull over and inspect your wiring. One of the inexpensive electrical "trouble-shooters" with the self-contained bulb that lights up when wiring is hot is worth buying and carrying.

Night riding apparel

Difficult as it is for other drivers to see you in the daytime, it is even more so at night. Wear light-colored or reflective clothing, and equip your cycle with plenty of reflectors on all sides if this has not already been done. I supplemented the factory-supplied reflectors on my cycle with some additional ones from the discount store. (See Chapter 3.) If your helmet does not feature reflective striping built-in, buy a roll of reflective tape and apply some prominently to your headgear. *Do not* apply fluorescent paint to your helmet.

Safety musts

Again, I urge you to avoid night riding as much as you can. It's more than normally dangerous. Eye pupil characteristics at night reduce to a large extent your ability to adjust to the glare of headlights and any "neon jungle" surrounding you. *Don't* try to compensate by the use of dark visor or any kind of colored glasses. Use a *clean, clear* visor. Never ride at night if you are drowsy, or have been drinking (in fact, don't ride under these conditions at *any time*). On rural roads and highways, riding at night gets even more risky. I doubt seriously if a good "reason why" case could ever be made in favor of any night riding for more than a few miles. Think about it.

13. The Importance of Weather

WHAT'S the safest way to ride in the rain? On snow or ice? In fog? The answer would be to take almost any vehicle other than a motorcycle. Motorcycles are actually *not* all-weather vehicles. Depending on where you live, there could be a few consecutive months when riding your cycle would be unwise. Wait till the nasty weather has moved on, and the streets are dry again. Just push your two-wheeler back under the carport, lock it, and use your car. After all, it needs to run out now and then, just to keep it in shape. If you don't have a car, it's a lot of fun to see just how much you can get for $400 or $500 when you're only looking for dependable bad-weather transportation and care little about the make, model or paint job.

Weather is vital to the cyclist because the motorcycle's design leaves it specially unsuited to slippery or rough surfaces. This fact is attested to by the large number of single-vehicle accidents involving motorcycles as compared to other types of vehicles. According to the Maryland study, an unusually high percentage of multiple vehicle accidents at rural, nonintersection locations are also caused by weather factors.

Watch weather changes

All of this makes it particularly important for you as a motorcycle rider to keep abreast of weather reports. Watch both the long-range and current weather forecasts, on TV, in the newspaper—and stay tuned to radio weathercasts when changes are likely.

Ride prepared

Try to avoid riding in the rain, but for those times when the weather man misses his no-rain forecast, try not to be caught totally unprepared. Trade off worn tires early, so that your treads will be at their best for slick surfaces. Carry a roll-up plastic wet suit on your cycle at all times, and slip into it quickly when rain starts while you are riding. If your gloves fail to give you positive hand control when wet, don't wear them in the rain. *Slow down* on the wet streets, and avoid the slick lane centers and paint stripes. Ditto for water puddles. Water splashed onto a hot engine, or a fall in water, can do a lot of damage. And, if it splashes away your visibility even for a moment, it could put you in real danger. Route yourself away from railroad tracks if you can. They're extra slick when wet. The same goes for construction sites, where trucks will be carrying mud onto the roadway.

Early rain hazard

Rain-slick surfaces are doubly dangerous for skidding potential within the first half-hour of the downpour, when loosened grease and dirt combine with rainwater for extra slipperiness. Pay special attention to keeping your machine straight up as you ride; and take the curves and corners nice and gentle. Take advantage of the tread tracks of cars in front of you, but don't follow too closely; give a wider separation than usual. Better still, pull off under some kind of shelter until the shower passes. (If there is lightning, stay out from under large trees.) After riding through water, check your brakes. Do it with a light touch, when you are clear of nearby traffic.

Rain affects vision

Vision becomes a special problem for the cyclist in the rain, because raindrops collect on your visor or goggles. Occasionally and carefully, you can make a quick hand-wipe that may help a little. If the problem is too bad, just stop and wait. I am able to see well enough through a rainy visor surface unless the density of the downpour is unusually heavy. As for the guy who doesn't wear a helmet, he's going to be in bad shape trying to squint through a pelting shower, or riding one-handed with the other shielding his eyes!

A 20-year-old rider on a 750 cc met his death in heavy rain on the Arkansas River bridge going into Fort Smith. He had overtaken and started to pass a car, and went left of the centerline to do it. What he couldn't see in that thick rain was an oncoming car that he struck head-on. The impact carried the rider back 129 feet, where he died beneath the car. His cycle skidded another 14 feet and bounced off the side of the highway.

Wind hazard

Strong side gusts of wind constitute another weather hazard for motorcycle operators, especially when either the rider, the cycle or both are lightweights. An example from the fatality files was an 11-year-old boy on a 125 cc bike. He managed to get several things going against him on his last ride: no license to ride, no tag on the cycle, no helmet on his head, surely too little experience, and speeding 10 miles per hour over the 35-miles-per-hour limit. But the thing that was his undoing, according to witnesses, was being hit by a heavy side wind. He lost control and lost his life.

My 200 cc bike is lighter than many street bikes, so I have a good deal of personal experience with problems from side winds and wind gusts. You *can* encounter stiff winds anywhere, so here are some tips to help you cope.

Coping with wind

There is a difference between wind gusts that come and go *suddenly*, and sustained heavy side wind pressure you have to deal with over a long period of time—hours on end during some highway trips. If the weather forecast calls for winds "gusting up to 35 miles per hour" or the like, you need to be ready for the quick shoves that start moving you out of your lane position, and may give you the feeling that your wheels are going to be jerked right out from under you. A primary problem here is being alert and quick to react, *without overcompensating* and winding up in a ditch. If you jerk back hard against a short-lived wind gust, you may have just that result. *Don't overcompensate* for wind gusts—and *don't* try *steering* against them. As in taking curves, your technique is *leaning* into the wind.

Your compensation for side winds is basically a matter of shifting your body weight. Simply dropping your shoulder on the side from which the wind is coming will do the trick of adding more body weight where it is needed, in a way that you can hold without fatigue for long stretches. On bikes as light as mine (250cc and under), I use a system of *relaxing* my handlebar grip on the side of the wind force, and "stiff-arming" the opposite grip. (I realize this sounds backward, but the side wind is trying to force the bike's front wheel *downwind*. On light bikes, I feel a need for both the body weight shift and the stiff-arm on the *downwind* side.) This is possible only for shorter rides; otherwise your stiff-arm would *get* that way. It will have no effect in steadying larger cycles, where body weight compensation is the only solution.

When leaning against heavy side winds, watch out for the sudden shift when you ride between the wind and such windbreaks as cuts through hills. The sudden absence of the wind force is like a reverse wind gust—like pressure from the *downwind* side of your machine.

There are times and places, of course, that are incompatible with motorcycling because of unreasonably heavy winds. Be smart enough to know when gales are making the traffic lanes unsafe for you. If you start out and get caught in a heavy windstorm, pull off in plenty of time and wait it out. Remember, motorcycles are not made for *all*-weather riding.

Winter hazards

As I mentioned earlier in Chapter 6, you need to sideline yourself during the days of snow and ice that winter brings to most of the country. Traction and visibility go down fast as temperatures plummet, car windows fog up, and skids become the order of the day. Motorists who couldn't see you in good weather certainly can't when they try to navigate through a snow-and-ice encrusted peephole on their front windshield. And because most of them really don't know how to handle their four-wheelers on slippery streets and roads, you just become more vulnerable than ever.

If the sun comes out following a period of snow and ice, don't be tempted to ride your cycle again as the icicles begin to fall. What you'll find is unexpected *patches* of ice (twice as slick at 30° as it is at zero) just where you need to apply your brakes—and motorists taking chances all around you as they forget about slippery overpasses, etc. There's a reason for that invariable rash of fender-benders in such conditions. Don't get involved. When you're sure your brakes won't freeze, and the riding surfaces are really dry, come out again.

14. Forget Your Right-of-way

YOU CAN have unquestioned legal right-of-way in any given traffic situation and wind up dead because you insisted on taking it. At any intersection, cross-traffic motorists can have a yield sign, a stop sign or a red signal light staring them in the face as you ride through with the right-of-way in your pocket. But *don't* think this guarantees they will *stop* for you.

Motorists aren't bad people, but all it takes for them to drive blithely past a stop sign into trouble is to be concentrating on something other than their driving, and it happens all the time. If they hit you, they may have to pay a heavy fine, and even lose their driver's license for a time. It may cause them plenty of mental anguish. But *you* may lose your life because you thought they *would* stop just because the sign *told* them to stop. Taking these things for granted is taking your *life* for granted.

That's why my safety formula for motorcycle riders is simply to *forget* your right-of-way. That does *not* mean sitting at an intersection like a dummy when it's "your turn" to go—you'd be holding up everybody doing that. What it *does* mean is forfeiting your legal rights in favor of protecting yourself if someone is intent on disregarding your right-of-way, for whatever reason. It just isn't worth risking your life to depend more on the protection of your right-of-way (purely *legal protection) than the super alertness and defensive riding that you can* depend on for survival.

Too few yielders

Statistics tell us two things about right-of-way problems and motorcycle accidents: (1) in most accidents involving a motorcycle and another vehicle, the primary error made by the operator at fault was *failure to yield*; and (2) the *motorist* was the operator most often at fault. In Chapter 11, a Motorcycle Safety Foundation study was cited to show that 90% of intersection clashes between a cycle and another vehicle were caused by failure to yield! It also stated that motorists failed to yield to motorcycles so often, it was their primary error 89% of the time. The same primary error was true of motorcycle operators 49% of the time.

From a practical safety standpoint, this tells you that your Number One intersection danger is any vehicle that can collide with you by failing to yield the right-of-way. Very often, this will be a motorist *on your left*, at right angles to you. The intersection may be open, giving you the right-of-way because you are on the motorist's right. It may be one that makes your lane through-traffic, with the motorist on your left facing a yield or stop sign. It may be a four-way stop intersection where you arrived first, and are entitled to proceed across the intersection first. Or it may be an intersection controlled by signal lights that are giving you the GO signal, and telling the motorist at your left to STOP. It doesn't matter in the least *how* you acquire the right-of-way. What does matter is that you can get killed by the guy at your left if he decides for any reason or *no* reason not to yield that right-of-way to you.

Watch the drivers

So, how do you *know* when this triple-threat is going to barge on across the intersection of your right-of-way? You don't. You *hesitate and watch him* until you believe he's harmless. Then you proceed with the kind of caution that says "I could be wrong about that guy 'staying hitched'; I'll be ready to take evasive action if he suddenly comes out of his position like a rodeo bronc out of a chute." This doesn't mean you need to take all day appraising the motorist and entering the intersection. You can also get into trouble in traffic by hesitating too long. It sometimes *encourages* a motorist to take your right-of-way. But if you do just that, *let* him take it. You don't need the right-of-way as much as you need your health.

Even though statistics most often place your intersection right-of-way problem at your left, it can be a vehicle at your right that illegally crosses your path. If such a motorist is moving straight across, you'll have just a bit more time to see what he's up to. If he wants to turn left in front of you, give him room. More often, the left-turner to beware will be an oncoming motorist facing you across the intersection. Remember, he may not signal his intentions in any way. To be safe, give *him* a signal to go ahead with his left turn if he appears to be stopped in the intersection for that purpose. It's best to let him clear before you go on across, removing him as a threat. If *you* wish to make a left turn while facing a motorist across an intersection, it again is wise to let him clear first, and make your left turn behind him.

A 31-year-old motorcyclist was riding at 55 miles per hour on Highway 66 when an oncoming woman driver turned left in front of him to enter a service station. After she had knocked the cyclist into the center of the highway, he was struck there by a third vehicle. His bike landed on the far side of the highway and he died two months later in the hospital. The citation the woman driver got for failure to yield the right-of-way didn't help him a bit.

One lesson to learn here is this: if there is a shopping center, service station or *any* driveway on your right, an oncoming car *can*—and someday *will*—make a left turn right into your path, intending to enter that driveway. As you face such oncoming drivers, cock your helmet slightly to the left, looking them straight in the eye. You may get some hint of their intentions before it is too late. *Be sure* your speed will allow you to stop if it becomes necessary in such an event. If there is another vehicle close behind you (and you'd better be aware of this), be ready to make an evasive move to the right or left, depending on the obstacles present.

Yield to foot traffic

Statistics also show that intersections are the most likely scenes of pedestrian injuries; and the most frequent motorcycle traffic violation, says the National Safety Council, is failure to yield right-of-way to a pedestrian or another vehicle. Keep an extra sharp watch on those afoot, whether they are in the proper crosswalk lanes, or jaywalking. Again it's more important to avoid an incident than it is to "be in the right." It's not easy to be in the right in an encounter with a pedestrian at an intersection. He has the legal right-of-way there. If you see a car come to a stop at an intersection, don't go on past him until you are certain there is no pedestrian or dog crossing in front of that car, and about to cross your path.

Yield to emergency vehicles

Along that line, never go around a vehicle that has slowed or stopped at an intersection while the traffic light gives a clear green, *until* you are sure the way is clear. This motorist may have heard or seen an emergency vehicle approaching in the cross-traffic. That emergency vehicle, of course, has the right-of-way over you at all times while they are "advertising" as the CB'ers put it—displaying a flashing light and/or signaling with siren or bell. If they are not signaling, but are proceeding as normal traffic, no right-of-way attaches to them. Don't forget to give proper right-of-way to school buses operating their warning signals during loading and unloading of students.

Watch parked cars

One last caution concerning a situation where you are likely to find your right-of-way infringed upon. When you are riding parallel to parked cars, be alert to one of them improperly entering traffic ahead of you. You can be missed easily in a rear-view mirror check by these motorists as they prepare to leave a parking spot. You and your bike fit very neatly into their blind spot.

The whole purpose of right-of-way is to help move traffic in an orderly manner, and to provide a means of fixing the blame in the event an accident occurs. When the driver of an automobile ran a stop sign in my city, a 17-year-old riding a 350 cc cycle was legally entering the intersection at right angles to the car. When the bike struck the car broadside, the young rider was ejected through the rear window of the car and slammed against the opposite door and window, killing him instantly. There was no difficulty establishing that he had the right-of-way, and that the motorist failed to yield. But that was the only easy thing about it.

Like every other vehicle operator legally on the streets and highways today, you will have right-of-way privileges as you ride your motorcycle. For safety's sake, use your right-of-way when all is clear; otherwise, *forget it.*

15. Seeing and Being Seen

JUDGING from voluminous accident reports, a rider on a motorcycle must have been the original "invisible man." Motorists can look directly at a cyclist and fail to see him. A highway patrol trooper demonstrated one reason for this, by asking me to hold a pencil about a foot in front of my eyes. "At the right distance," he said, "an oncoming cyclist can be hidden from your view behind that pencil!" I could see that he was right. Even broadside to a motorist, we are difficult to *perceive* when motorists are basically looking out for other vehicles their own size. Hopefully this will change for the better as motorcycles continue to increase in numbers. But for now, ride with the knowledge that the only thing you have to do to become invisible is to get on your bike.

When I first started riding, a fellow square dancer admitted that he had once failed to see a cyclist in traffic, "and I was looking right at him!" I found it hard to believe; but not too many months later a driver almost ran me down two blocks from my home—the camper driver mentioned in an earlier chapter. He claimed he positively didn't see me until I veered 90° and 25 feet out of my way evading him. Impossible or not, you and I have to proceed on the assumption that we *can't* be seen by at least some motorists, then do everything possible to make sure we *are seen*, and that we can see.

According to the Motorcycle Safety Foundation, a big reason for many intersection accidents involving a motorcycle and another vehicle is the smaller size of the cycle/rider unit (harder to see)—and also the greater difficulty motorists have in judging cycle speeds. Well, if they can't see us or judge our speed when they do, it becomes our responsibility to see *them*, and exercise proper speed control at all times.

Give your eyes a break

Since you are betting your life on your eyes, take good care of them while you ride. Wear a helmet with a clean visor or good pair of cyclist goggles. Your visor needs to be large enough to give you all of the peripheral vision you have. When it accumulates too many scrapes and scratches, get rid of the visor and replace it.

Bright sun is a hazard

Motorists driving into the bright sun really have a tough time seeing you, and the same problem exists in reverse. As soon as you are capable of one-hand operation (something I would never recommend as a riding style), use one hand just for a split second when you need to shield out strong sun rays to give you the lay of the traffic. You may need to do this more than once, but only very quickly each time; both of your hands normally belong on the grips. But I would rather use the quick hand-shield and know what I'm heading into, than blindly ride into an area of glare and hope for the best.

I prefer the dark ("smoke") visor for daytime cycling, to help combat sun glare. Keep a clear visor to snap on for the few times you find night riding necessary; or keep an extra helmet on hand with a clear shield. If you don't use the helmet shield, sunglasses may seem more comfortable than goggles. But they don't give as much protection; and they let the wind stream across your eyes, causing tears to form. Not the best thing in the world for your vision. If you have no visor on your helmet, sunglasses will probably be illegal as eye protection.

Keep it clean

Whatever form your eye protection takes, bugs will splatter against it now and then. Stop and clean your face shield or goggles as soon as possible. *Don't* try maintaining full speed while you guide your bike with one hand and flick at the bug's remains with the other. When you get too many such flying objects, your shield will need replacing. Bugs not only splatter, they scratch the plastic permanently.

Rear-view mirrors

While seeing where you're headed is the most important thing, knowing what's headed for *you* is a close second. You need two rear-view mirrors, properly adjusted to give you a wide sweep of vision behind you, and as much of the immediate traffic to either side of you in a close proximity as is compatible with the good rear view. If one mirror gets broken, don't think you can do fine with the other. And *don't* use chopped-up X-design mirrors or any others that provide inadequate vision. Rear-views are tools, not toys or decorations.

Use those rear-view mirrors frequently. Always check them when you are coming to an intersection stop. Don't keep your eyes on them long, of course, but glance often enough to know at all times what's going on back there. Again, keep in mind that vehicles behind you are always *closer* than they appear to be in your mirrors. *Learn the difference!*

Weather and visibility

Bad weather means bad vision and bad visibility—another good reason to park your bike and take your car. Rain and fog cut down on your ability to see, and the ability of motorists to see you. Winter weather produces breath-fogged interiors on auto glass, and exterior windshield surfaces that are iced over, with only peephole-sized scrapings relied on by motorists.

A 17-year-old was riding his 750 cc cycle on fog-damp streets when he made a fatal move. He was in the process of passing one car going his same direction, and had just about completed it as he moved into a clear intersection. But the intersection didn't remain clear; a second vehicle appeared suddenly out of the fog, going in the opposite direction, and just as suddenly turned left into the cyclist. He was trapped between the turning car and the one he had just passed, and didn't come out alive.

No see, no pass

The National Safety Council says "if you can't see ahead, don't try to pass." This young man combined that error with the poor visibility risk of the fog, and violation of the rule about not passing within 100 feet of an intersection. If the cyclist wasn't aware he was that near an intersection, that is also because of the unsafe visibility in the fog. The "no see, no pass" advice also applies to entering a trafficway from a driveway or parking lot. If trees, construction, parked cars, etc. make it impossible for you to see all of the approaching traffic, ease into a position where you *can* see before you pass.

Rule to memorize

The rule to memorize in connection with vision and visibility is simple but vital: *Anytime, anywhere* you find it difficult or impossible to see for a safe distance in all directions, *reduce your speed and increase your alertness.*

Lane position

A big part of seeing and being seen in traffic depends on your positioning on the roadway as you ride. Chapter 16 will cover lane position factors in detail; but a couple of things obviously need to be mentioned here. Spend as little time as possible behind trucks or other vehicles that are hard to see around. With the right amount of space between you and the vehicle ahead, this problem will be lessened, and positioning yourself behind side-mounted rear-view mirrors on trucks also helps. If you can't see the rear-view mirror of a vehicle ahead, the driver can't see you. And it's better to ride either left (preferred) or right of lane center to improve your own ability to see ahead.

Riding in the blind spots of a vehicle ahead makes for a bad scene; and all vehicles have them. Remember the time when you were driving your car, and a motorcycle cop appeared suddenly alongside before you had any inkling he was in the vicinity? That officer and his Harley-Davidson Electra-Glide make an even bigger impression on the scenery than you will on your smaller street bike. So, you can realize how true it is about that blind spot problem. Position yourself such that every vehicle near you at least has the opportunity to see you—or pull back a safe distance.

Dress to be seen

In your efforts to be seen by motorists, there are a few practical things you can do. It helps to wear light, bright-colored—even reflective—clothing. Inexpensive reflective tape applied to your cycle jacket as well as the cycle itself is useful for night riding. One more good reason for wearing a helmet is the quick identification it gives to surrounding traffic that there is a motorcycle rider in their midst. Certain color combinations including reflective striping give even more visibility to your helmet. Mine is white with red and blue luminescent stripes that gleam brightly in the glare of car lights at night. If you regularly carry a package satchel on your back, stick some reflective tape on it for even greater visibility.

Aid from reflectors

Make sure there are plenty of side reflectors on your bike; the bicycle supplies section of your discount store or variety store will have some inexpensive types that work fine. Place them so they will be clear of your body and visible while you ride.

Use the lights

Lights on your motorcycle provide one of the best means of being seen. Regardless of what the law in your state says about daytime use of your lights, *put them on!* If yours come on automatically when you switch on the ignition, fine. If not, make it a habit to do it yourself every time you start up. Don't worry about using up your battery or bulbs. Without those lights to help motorists see you coming, you may use up your life too quickly.

Make sure all your lights work properly, and keep the covers clean. The New York Port Authority has found from experience that cars and trucks have fewer accidents when drivers put on their lights, even in daytime. It's doubly valid for motorcycles. I have mentioned flashing your brake light as a warning to motorists behind that you are slowing or stopping, and they are overtaking you too fast. It has really worked remarkably well for me; most drivers seem to know immediately what I am communicating, and they usually respond well. If you habitually "ride your brake," you'll not only confuse motorists but lose the benefit of the warning device. Like "crying wolf," it can be done once too often.

Besides your headlight and tail/brake light, you have turn-signal lights. Since most of them are not automatic, signaling your turns is your personal responsibility. Don't shirk it by turning without signaling. You could rightfully be sued for negligence over an accident caused when you failed to signal—*if* you came out alive.

Always signal well in advance of your turn—more so on the highway than in the city. You can use hand signals instead of lights; and you can combine the two if you like. Make sure you have practiced the hand signals carefully before you do this one-handed act in traffic. It isn't difficult; but it does require practice. In using turn-indicator lights, remember to cancel them after your turn (I usually do it *before* the turn is complete) to avoid confusion on the part of motorists.

You can be heard

Stern disciplinarians once told their children they should "be seen and not heard." On a motorcycle, be sure you are both seen *and* heard. Get those air horns, keep them in working order, and use them, right along with your lights. Just one thing: ride as though you are invisible and mute. Never *depend* on being seen *or* heard in traffic.

16. About Lane Position

ONE OF the prime reasons many motorists are hostile to cyclists is because of a few reckless riders. These are the ones who think the compact size and flexibility of the cycle gives them license to dart in and out among the cars and trucks. I couldn't agree more with the motorists. These darting idiots not only risk their own necks with thoughtless abandon, but other lives as well—and give *all* cycle riders a bad name in the process.

For safety's sake, don't abuse the unique mobility that enables you to squeeze through narrow spaces, and move like a purple martin on the wing. Reserve it for emergency evasive maneuvers; and treat traffic lane positioning as you would in an automobile. If any lane maneuver would cause you to be subject to arrest as the driver of a car, *don't do it* on a cycle. This isn't just a suggestion. As mentioned in Chapter 9, you are subject to the same traffic laws and safety rules as a motorist.

In the motorcycle accident research sponsored by the Motorcycle Safety Foundation, lane usage (or *mis*usage) was the second highest basic control task by the motorcycle operator responsible for accidents.

Which lane?

Certain lane positions make it easier for the motorcyclist to see and be seen. This lane choice can vary with changes in roadway conditions, traffic flow and maneuvers. All signs, roadway markings and control signals need to be understood and observed. Control personnel (construction area flagmen, traffic officers, etc.) traffic commands must be obeyed.

In positioning yourself in a lane of traffic, make sure you can be seen by the motorist ahead, in his rear-view mirror. Even though you would be visible when exactly centered behind the vehicle, avoid this location because of the oil accumulation hazard encountered there. Normal preference should go to the *left wheel track position,* which discourages motorists from overtaking you by crowding in alongside on your left. Move *right* of center, of course, before making a right turn. If you are being passed on the left, you can move to the center of your lane until the passing maneuver is complete, then move back.

Never ride in a motorist's blind spot if you can avoid it. If you find yourself there, change your speed, lane position or both to become "visible" again. Moving to right or left within a lane can also serve to put more lateral safety space between you and a hazard on either side.

The left wheel track suggestion is for your position within a traffic lane. As for which individual lane to select, keep in mind the general rule, *"Keep right except when passing."* This normal preference would put you in the lane nearest the curb or shoulder while maintaining a speed within the legal maximum and minimum, and experiencing no need to pass other vehicles.

To pass someone in that outside lane, you would move into the left lane when four lanes are present (two each way), or into the middle lane on a six-lane stretch (three each direction). The inside (farthest left) lane would be used for the maximum speed, and for passing vehicles in the other lane or lanes. On a four-lane thoroughfare (two each way), I sometimes ride in this inside lane if a broad median separates me from oncoming traffic, and visibility is poor at intersections on my right.

When traffic going your direction has a choice of three lanes, as on a six-lane highway, cruising at the right puts you farthest away from that "hot," maximum-speed traffic at the center of the roadway. If there is a broad median between the two inside lanes, you may be tempted to cruise inside and either move over into the middle lane when someone wants to pass—or let *him* find a passing space in the middle lane. Neither choice is the smartest move you can make. The speed drivers consider the inside lane *theirs*—and this includes not only cruise-control maximum-legal drivers, but those who see fit to overrule the 55-miles-per-hour law with a CB-cleared 75.

It isn't easy to judge approach speeds in your rear-view, and these illegally fast overtakers can spell big trouble. Also, the more lane changes you make to give way for passers, the more chances for a mishap. At those speeds, mishaps are usually fatal for cyclists.

As for the center lane, you are literally "surrounded" by traffic on both sides, approaching or being approached at greatly different speeds and passing through blind spots in relation to your cycle. You are in double jeopardy from abrupt lane-changers as well; they can come at you from either side. Even if your speed more nearly matches the center-lane traffic, you'll be safer on the outside during long open stretches.

On four-lane city streets, I find another advantage in occupying the righthand lane: so much left turning goes on in busy traffic. These are not only wasteful of your time, but dangerous. So many motorists give no signal, and others decide so suddenly there is little time to read their minds. If you need to make a left turn, move into the left lane well in advance of the location.

Using the righthand lane does involve its own set of risks for the cyclist, and you need to keep them in mind. You are closer to parked cars; watch them carefully, and be alert for dogs or children darting out from behind them. Cars entering your four-lane street from your right are closer; you will have less visibility and shorter reaction time for them.

Don't crowd

This is a good place to remind you not to be a tailgater. Give plenty of space to yourself for reaction and maneuvering time between you and the nearest car ahead. Following too close to a left-lane motorist while you occupy the righthand lane will put you in his blind spot. Keep your distance, and be alert for any move the left-lane motorist might make to move into your lane.

Use your mirrors

In any lane, keep monitoring your rear-view mirrors by frequent quick glances while you keep a straight course; and by a fast head-check before you make a lane-changing move on your own. You need to have the lane knowledge required for swift evading action, should an oncoming vehicle suddenly swerve left in front of you. This maneuver happens so often it's classic.

Riding with others

If you are riding with a buddy, do *not* ride abreast of each other. One should take the lead in the left-third lane position; the other goes behind and to the right. This avoids contact problems in the event of wind gusts or other emergencies. If you are in a group of riders, this staggered formation should be followed for every pair. Leave space between each pair of riders for overtaking cars to pull in safely. *Do not* block the highway so as to interfere with traffic.

Times to change lanes

Besides lane changes necessitated by right or left turns, passing slow traffic and giving yourself more lateral maneuvering room between you and potential hazards, there are other valid times to make lane changes. As you ride on crosstown expressways in city areas, or on interstate highways with limited access, you need to keep a sharp eye on merging traffic at entrance ramps. If you can see that an entering vehicle will need your lane to move into smoothly just about the time you would arrive at the merge point, a *safe* lane change to the left could be in order.

If you are passing a slow vehicle, and see an impatient motorist go left of center in a passing maneuver of his own, your best quick decision may be to change lanes again, going back where you started. This will require you to be aware of overtaking traffic in the right-hand lane, and to make a controlled reduction of speed, dropping behind the car you had been passing. Even so, it is probably a better option than speeding up to *hopefully* complete your passing attempt before you lock horns with the oncoming passer. That would put two speeding vehicles in a head-on path for at least a few seconds, and those seconds could spell disaster.

The roadway itself can force you into lane changing—by such things as a reduction in the number of lanes, permanently or on an emergency basis. Obstacles ahead in the outside lane can force you into the left lane. Should your recognition of the need for a lane change be slow, the maneuver itself may become something of an emergency. In that event, "out-tracking" can provide the needed speed. (Yes, this is the same type of move you've probably resented in little old ladies who often curve left before making a right turn, and vice versa.) You just lean away from the direction of your intended turn, then back into it. *Caution:* This is *not* a proper maneuver without proper signaling, or if you haven't mastered it first. In practicing it, work up gradually from a slow beginning speed.

One further caution would be to make good head-checks of nearby traffic *before* making lane-change decisions. Make absolutely sure the way is clear for the amount of time you will need. This involves accurately estimating the speed of overtaking and oncoming vehicles, and starting your move early. If you're not good at estimating, give yourself more room to operate in, even if you delay yourself and others doing it. A recent motorcycle death happened locally when the cyclist turned left in front of an oncoming truck without sufficient working room.

Be sure to signal

Another responsibility of yours in lane changing is to *signal* your intentions. The fact that too many people are apathetic about signaling today is no excuse for adding to their numbers. A 17-year-old 360 cc

bike operator pulled an "out-tracking" maneuver from a righthand
lane position as an overtaking car started to pass. The rider was the
only one who knew he intended to outtrack slightly, then make a U-
turn. He made no signal, leaving the overtaking motorist completely
uninformed. The result is easy to guess—another fatality. Signaling
is *more* than a responsibility; it's a survival aid.

Times not to change lanes

In Chapter 9, I related a personal experience that taught me a time
not to change lanes. Don't change lanes with the illegal intent to
cross a highway median at an unauthorized location. It can get you
splattered by a speeding overtaker who won't believe you would
make such a dumb move; it happened to me. What I should have
done—the lesson I learned the hard way—was to use the authorized
median crossing point about a half-mile farther down the highway.
Changing lanes just for the *heck* of it is also hazardous, because it's
confusing to other motorists; and when nearby motorists get confused, you can get hurt. Find the lane most compatible with your
speed and upcoming plans, and settle down in it nice and steady.
Change lanes only when there's a need, and make your intentions
known to everyone.

Other lane changers

We've discussed times to change lanes and times not to change
lanes. There is also a time to be alert for *other* lane-changers. Do you
know when this is true? If your answer is *all the time*, go to the head
of the class. Some times are more logical than others; but you can be
confronted with a lane-changer when you would least expect it, and
that vehicle can be twice as dangerous as the one you anticipate.

When you are riding in any passing lane, look for lane-changers to
crowd in on you when things begin to bottleneck up ahead. The
same thing will happen when a large or slow-moving vehicle shows
up in the lane to your right. Other traffic overtaking such a vehicle in
that lane will pull left into your lane to pass. They have three
choices: (1) speed up and enter your lane in front of you; (2) reduce
speed and pull in behind you; or (3) pull left without looking at or

seeing you, exactly where you are riding. Choices 1 and 3 can mean real trouble for you. *Keep alert.*

Emergency changes

No matter which lane you are occupying, a stalled car ahead in the same lane will precipitate lane switching, some of it frantic and hazardous to you.

An overtaking emergency vehicle will cause other vehicles around you to change lanes in an attempt to get out of its way. Make sure they don't create another emergency by running over you in the process; and be sure you don't move in the wrong direction to make way for the emergency vehicle. At times, the driver of such a vehicle will decide to pass on your *right*, rather than try to cope with heavy traffic ahead on your left. *Swivel your head* to help you make the right choice of evasive actions. You need to know exactly what is going on.

Watch *oncoming* drivers who decide on a passing maneuver. Some of them think nothing of crossing the centerline into your lane in order to gain wide clearance of the vehicle they are passing. At such a time you had better be well aware of traffic conditions close behind you. Evading the centerline crosser could throw you directly into the path of a car overtaking on your right.

If you are in a heavy group of traffic as your roadway narrows from four lanes to two, or funnels you into a detour, take care not to get yourself trapped by vehicles changing lanes of necessity.

Riding between lanes

Riding *between* traffic lanes is simply asking for trouble. You are riding in blind spots, and you are riding into positions too close to vehicles in adjacent lanes for any kind of safety. Between two moving lanes, vehicles can turn into you from either direction before you have time to react evasively. Between a moving lane and a line of parked vehicles, you risk getting a door opened in your face, or having one of the parked cars pull out suddenly in front of you. And because it's an illegal maneuver, you always risk a traffic fine as your minimum problem.

Shoulder riding

Riding on shoulders compares closely to riding between lanes. In both cases, it's possible to do on a motorcycle; but neither practice is safe, smart or legal. Shoulders are not motorcycle paths; they are emergency stopping zones. If you try saving time by passing a long line of motorists on the right, using the shoulder area, an impatient motorist may suddenly pull off to make an emergency stop. Keep in mind at all times that you are subject to the *same traffic rules that apply to motorists.* That means among other things, *don't* try to turn shoulders into private freeways.

Watch the signs

You need to do this at all times, of course. But specifically in connection with your lane position, there will be signs warning you in advance if you will be required to change lanes ahead. If you are riding on an expressway routing through traffic around a city, you will either be continuing on via the same highway, changing to another at a junction, or exiting for a local destination. Any of these choices calls for concentration in fast traffic, to maneuver into the proper lane at the right time. If the route is familiar, you will know how long you can remain in the faster lanes before moving into position for an exit or change of direction. If it is unfamiliar, give every sign a good visual check and move into the proper lane as early as possible. Forced last-minute lane changes in high-speed traffic are murder.

In more localized traffic patterns, keep an eye out for one-way street beginning and ending points; signs limiting left turns to certain hours of the day; signs permitting "right turns on red after stop," or stating "no turns on red"; signs requiring you to travel an additional block before turning in the direction you wish to go; signs calling for lane-changing or detours around construction; and on and on. Signs making changes in the traffic flow, and requiring you to make unanticipated lane changes, can sprout up with no notice except in and of themselves. The only safe answer is constant alertness, and early maneuvering to comply with such signs. Be alert, too, for the nearby motorist who notes a traffic sign at the last moment and makes a quick compliance maneuver *directly at you.*

17. Alertness is Everything

OF ALL the things you can do to stay out of trouble on a motorcycle, *total alertness* is probably the most vital. The mere fact that 72% of all multi-vehicle accidents are caused by a cycle striking the other vehicle, indicates a high degree of cyclist inattention.

Total alertness involves the full use of all your faculties to tell you when something is wrong, or may soon be. Not just your eyes and ears, but even your "sixth sense" if you have one, must be fully operative. Riding a motorcycle is no place to put your feet up and relax as though you were home in your favorite easy chair. It's a place to *concentrate* and *anticipate.* It is a place to know everything going on about you, and all that *might* happen under an unbelievable variety of circumstances that would give you little concern driving a car. And every minute you operate a cycle, you must hold yourself "on guard"—ready to react properly to any situation that could put your safety in jeopardy.

Alcohol or drugs are taboo

One point already covered in Chapter 5 needs to be mentioned again as we consider the importance of staying totally alert. *You cannot safely ride a cycle while under the influence of alcohol or drugs.* Need another fatality report to convince you? Here's one. A 27-year-old riding a 250 cc bike had too many things going against him. He had been drinking and he was riding at night on city streets without a helmet. His speed of 40 miles per hour may even have been legal where he was riding; many city streets permit it. But this young man was thrown to his death when he struck a curb—due to "inattention," said the official report. I wouldn't argue with that conclusion. How *could* he give proper attention and alertness to the task of operating his cycle safely when his faculties had been dulled by alcohol?

Constant eye-scan

In the motorcycle accident research study done by BioTechnology, Inc., of Virginia, surveillance by the rider tied for second place in safety importance. And the kind of constant eye-scan surveillance that will save your life must be based on alertness that lasts as long as your hand is on the throttle.

Worst hazard hours

The National Safety Council has even segregated the time when you need to be most alert on a cycle. Studies reported to them from various states show that motorcycles are involved in more accidents between 3 P.M. and 7 P.M. Saturday is the worst day and, of course, the summer months (June, July and August) log more cycle accidents than others. This doesn't mean you can drop your guard at other hours, on other days, in other months. Alertness is a full-time job if you want to ride safely. But you might be exceptionally careful in the afternoon and early evening hours.

Hazard examples

Three basic groups of hazards must command your attention while riding: (1) other vehicles; (2) pedestrians and animals; and (3) immobile objects. To give proper attention to all three groups, you have to keep your head up and your eyes moving, including frequent glances at your rear-view mirrors.

Even though you and your cycle are not included in any of the three hazard groups mentioned, it definitely is a part of alertness to know what is going on with regard to your own bike. One 19-year-old riding a 250 cc rode off down the street unaware that he had left his kickstand down. Nothing happened while he proceeded on the straight and level; but when he took a left curve at only 20 miles per hour, the kickstand struck the street and threw the cycle out of control. It went up over the curb and slid 22 feet. The rider was taken to three different hospitals in four days before he died of the injuries sustained in this "freak" accident.

Putting your kickstand up before taking off should be as automatic as turning your ignition key. But making procedures automatic should never eliminate your conscious awareness that each step in the sequence has been done. If doing things automatically is unsafe for you, check them off each time *by the numbers*.

Constant concentration is a must for the cyclist because operating a motorcycle is a more difficult job than driving a car. Just maintaining your balance while you are alert to traffic conditions around you makes it so. You can be thrown simply by crossing railroad tracks the wrong way; or by encountering an oil slick or chuckhole. The subject of surface hazards is covered in detail in Chapter 6. Review it periodically until surface surveillance becomes a well-established riding habit.

The more you ride in traffic and study the movements of drivers around you, the better you will become in predicting maneuvers before they happen. I am referring to such practices as a motorist ahead in your lane pulling slightly to the right, inviting you to pass—or pulling toward the centerline to warn you *not* to pass yet. The problem with "anticipating the command" is the chance that you might read a motorist's actions the wrong way now and then. And it takes only one time to put you in the hospital. The safest policy for the cyclist is to hold himself in readiness for an expected maneuver, while proceeding only on the basis of what he sees actually taking place. There is a valid use of anticipating certain actions from conditions observed; these will be covered later in the chapter.

Check all of the traffic

Total alertness calls for concentration on other traffic ahead, to the right and left, and overtaking vehicles to the rear. You must keep your eyes moving to accomplish this, not resting on any one scene more than a couple of seconds. You must support this continuous eye movement with frequent head checks, swiveling your neck right and left as far as necessary to get the complete picture of surrounding traffic. Use your rear-view mirrors regularly, particularly before making a move from one lane position to another.

Watch intersect points

Keep close check on roadway locations where other vehicles can intersect your path of travel (intersections, private drives and other entrance/exit points, railway crossings, off-street parking lots and shopping centers, etc.). A 35-year-old rider on a 450 cc cycle was killed while riding on a U.S. highway with his brother. The brother rode a 650 cc. Both men were traveling at the legal 55-miles-per-hour speed, and were aware of an upcoming intersection with a county road. What they *didn't* see was a convertible being driven by a woman under the influence of alcohol, as it entered the highway from an angling private driveway near the intersection.

When the cyclist riding the 450 cc bike saw the car emerge swiftly onto the highway in front of him, he laid down 84 feet of skid marks to the point of impact. He was knocked back three feet and killed; his brother, who had no time to brake, was thrown over the convertible, but lived. Partial cloudiness may have helped obscure the driveway. Reduced speed and total alertness by the cyclists could have prevented the tragedy.

True, the woman driver was negligent in this case. True, the American Motorcycle Association has published statistics showing that more than 70% of all accidents between motorcycles and automobiles are the fault of the *motorist*. This is absolutely no consolation to us who ride cycles. It simply reinforces my advice to you about your relationship with automobiles in traffic: *expect* the motorist to do the wrong thing—to look at you without seeing you; to ignore your signal light right-of-way; to turn left in front of you with no turn signal; to drink and drive in a reckless manner. Then ride accordingly.

Expect failure to yield

Nationally, statistics show that it is the *motorist* who fails to yield. Take your safety cue from this fact. Don't expect him to yield to you;

statistics already prove he won't. Again, statistics show that if an improper turn causes a car-cycle accident, it is the *motorist* who usually makes the illegal turn. Why expect him to turn properly, when the records say he won't? The Maryland study revealed a high number of accidents caused when motorists crossed the centerline. Keep alert to this possibility. More than half of the time when failure to stop or control a vehicle is involved, it is the motorist who is at fault. I don't know what this says to you, but to me, it says don't trust the motorist to stop when he should, or always be in proper control of his vehicle. Cold, recorded facts prove this.

So, a part of total alertness riding is watching other vehicles around you with the proven knowledge that all too often the drivers will do the wrong thing—and *you* will be the one most likely to suffer for it if an accident results.

Watch those signs

Watching all official signs on, above and at the side of your roadway is a part of being totally alert. They tell you what you are expected to do at given locations, and what other vehicles around you may be expected to do. (Again, don't commit your life to a conviction that other vehicle operators will always obey these signs. Wait to see what they *are* going to do before making your own move.)

Watch parked cars

Being alert to other vehicles includes keeping a careful eye on parked and other non-moving vehicles. If there is a driver in a car, it can become a moving vehicle at any moment, often when you least expect it. If you can't see whether there is a driver in the vehicle, don't take chances. Treat it as something that can go into motion suddenly, without notice. Watch for any tell-tale exhaust smoke or car movement in every line of parked vehicles.

The same alert attitude should pertain to parked cars regarding the door-opening possibilities. As a bicycle rider at a younger age, my biggest problem seemed to be getting knocked flat on the street by some parked motorist who decided to get out just as I wheeled by. The problem is still there for the motorcycle rider.

Riding behind trucks

Riding behind trucks is something to avoid in any case, if only for
the visibility limitation it causes. But when you see one carrying a
poorly loaded cargo of junk, tree limbs or anything else that could
bounce off, lose him at the first opportunity. Give him lots of lead
distance until you have a chance to pass.

Pesky pets

Animals are also worthy of your concentration as you ride totally
alert. The Maryland study established encounters with domestic animals as a primary cause of single-vehicle motorcycle accidents. It
doesn't pay to kick at dogs chasing you. You might twist your turning wheel abruptly and lose your balance in doing so. Don't run in
front of a car in another lane trying to avoid the pesky pet, either.
Just move out of range quickly, first reducing your speed, then accelerating swiftly. You may prefer to stop and dismount to deal with
him, depending on your appraisal of the animal.

You can save a child

Keep very alert for children as you ride. They are too young to realize
the danger of on-street playgrounds. Within a single month in my
city, a boy was killed by a car when he skateboarded down a driveway
into the street from behind a parked car; and a 3-year-old girl on a
tricycle pedaled out of a downtown alley into the street and was run
down by a woman driver who never saw her. I have had to blast my
air horns to warn skateboarders who were riding into the street after
dark—no reflective materials anywhere, and parents seemingly obliv-
ious to their activities. Children running, riding "big wheels," or bi-
cycling are equally hazardous. Only your alertness can save them—
and yourself.

Stationary hazards

Stationary objects, too, are hazards for the cyclist. When hedgerows,
trees, buildings, junk cars or anything else crowds the roadway on
either side, *slow down*. You can't see around or through such ob-

structions; so you can't know when a car, child or pet will come rushing from behind them into your path. *Anytime, anywhere* you find it difficult or impossible to see for a safe distance in all directions—this is the time and place to reduce your speed and increase your alertness. Other immobile objects such as bridges and guard rails can be hazardous in themselves unless you give them plenty of room. Be alert to their proximity as you ride past, and slow down if that is needed to help you gauge accurately.

Ride ahead

"THINK AHEA$_D$" became a familiar sign over the past decade. A two-word sign we cycle riders need to frame between our handlebars is "RIDE AHEAD." This does *not* mean to ignore conditions right where you are at any given moment. It would be ridiculous to be alert to a possible left-turner a block ahead, while a car on your immediate right is about to wheel out of a drive and put tread marks down your back. But it *is* smart to *know about* the guy a block ahead who appears to be a candidate for turning left in front of you. As you ride, keep every possible hazard within the upcoming full city block under constant surveillance. This, combined with that all-important reaction space you keep between you and the next vehicle ahead, will go a long, long way toward making you that modern miracle: a two-wheeler operator who has never had an accident.

Expect these hazards

In the section dealing with the concentration required for total alertness, I mentioned that *anticipation* is also valid in certain circumstances. Here are a few to remember:

1. An out-of-state vehicle ahead of you may get confused as you approach an intricate intersection. Keep your distance and be prepared to change your speed and/or lane suddenly if the out-of-stater makes a late-decision maneuver.

2. Children are playing ahead in an off-street area. Be alert for a possible dash into the street for a ball, frisbee, etc.

3. Exhaust fumes are coming from a parked car, and the wheels are turned toward the street. Be ready for a move into traffic without warning. (The only place you see a motorist signal before pulling away from a curb is at the driver's license examinations.)

4. A car at right angles to your riding lane is rapidly approaching a stop or yield sign that is in your favor. Proceed towards the intersection *expecting* him to run the sign. Better to anticipate the worst and be fooled by a tire-screeching stop, than to enter the intersection with the law on your side and a traffic violator on your neck.

5. An oncoming vehicle is going into a turn that lies between it and you, at a speed too fast for safety. Check your rearview quickly, reduce your speed, and get ready for unwanted company as he is forced to violate the centerline.

6. A driver ahead of you, going the same direction, impatiently starts to pass a second car on a hill. Be alert to the strong possibility that an oncoming car will top the rise and force the passer to cut back suddenly. If this happens, he can cause a careening accident with the car being passed, or jam his vehicle into your path while slowing— possibly causing you to overrun him, *unless* your alertness in anticipating the hazard saves you.

7. A driver ahead is weaving from lane to lane or otherwise driving erratically. Stay away from him until you can safely get away from him.

8. Exhaust vapors suddenly become visible from the tailpipe of the car ahead. This can be your first indication of a slowing action that will require *you* to reduce your speed accordingly.

9. An oncoming vehicle is closing fast on a second vehicle stopped in the roadway. Be ready for the possibility that the closing vehicle will swerve across the centerline quickly

and try to cut back in front of you, back into his proper lane.

10. The car ahead flashes its brake lights. Slow down and be alert for anything.

11. A nearby vehicle has windows that are steamed or frosted over. Be alert to the fact that you are now *doubly* invisible to this driver.

12. You see a slight movement in a streetside door of a parked car. Be alert to someone alighting from the car into your riding lane as you pass.

13. A same-direction vehicle is driving alongside you. Its driver gives no sign of altering his speed or direction as you both approach a point where his lane merges into yours. Be alert to the good chance he will cut suddenly in front of you just before reaching the merge point.

14. A pedestrian is walking toward an intersection briskly. The signal light is red to him and green to you; but he is looking at a pretty girl, not the signal. Be alert to the possibility you will have to give way to him to avoid an encounter.

15. A school bus is parked on the opposite side of the street from you. Off-street on the right, children are approaching. Alertness will tell you there could be a traffic conflict if the children start running to cross the street and board the bus. Proceed accordingly.

In each of the above examples, you are anticipating something that hasn't happened, and may *not* happen. But as an alert motorcycle rider, you can't look upon this as "borrowing trouble." Instead, realize that you are taking an extra step to *prevent* trouble. It's worth it.

Prompt reactions

Total alertness—concentrating and anticipating—involves diagnosing trouble before it happens. It also involves prompt reaction when trouble *does* happen. If your throttle sticks, alertness enables you to flip the red kill switch instantly. If a clutch cable suddenly gives way in traffic, alertness tells you instantly what has happened and what to do about it (again, kill the engine and apply both brakes with caution dictated by your traffic situation). Whatever emergency arises, you will be better prepared to cope with it if you are *alert to its possibility.*

Have options ready

A cyclist should ride along asking himself a constant stream of questions such as: *"What if* that woman turns in front of me to enter the shopping center parking lot to my right—and does it with no warning? What can I do? Can I stop safely without being hit from behind? Can I veer left to miss her, since no one is following her? Would I head off the possibility of her left turn by sounding my horn?"

Changes can bring hazards

Cyclists must also be alert to changing conditions that require changing tactics for the sake of safety. If a highway that has been comparatively straight and level takes on a mountainous complexion with numerous curves and downgrades followed quickly by steep climbs, you must be quick to adjust to the new hazards of the road. If the weather suddenly worsens, bringing on artificial darkness and slick surfaces, or heavy wind gusts with blowing dust and sand, you need to get off the roadway as soon as possible and take shelter until riding conditions again permit alertness.

You need to quickly sense changing traffic patterns at certain hours of the day in the city, and at close proximity to cities as you move in on a highway. You need to be alert to the difference in the way "country folks" drive, compared to the disciplined traffic flow in the city. You need to be alert to such changes and differences, and adjust your riding method quickly to mesh safely with these changes.

Safe riding requires many skills at different times; but one skill is *always* used: on a motorcycle, *alertness!*

18. Watch Those Turners!

WHEN THE various state highway patrol departments issue their annual motorcycle accident reports, the improper turn is usually right at the top of the list of collision causes. Usually, this maneuver and "failure to yield" are the two leading accident causes. It's safe to say that the classic motorcycle fatality results when a motorist makes a left turn into a cyclist.

The lesson to be learned is apparent. Beware of improper turners and refuse to become a classic cycle-auto crash victim. "Forewarned is forearmed," goes the old saying. Act on it and stay alive.

Turners do give clues

As you ride, you *must* stay alert for the motorist about to make a turn. Unfortunately, this can by *any* of them; and you'll need to develop a skilled eye for the signs indicating when it's about to happen. Don't expect that sign to be the legally required turn signal, flashing for all the world to see. You'll need to learn how to read minute car and driver movements and employ "eyeball interaction" if you're close enough. Sometimes, at least, a motorist will actually look in the direction of his turn before he starts it, giving you a needed advance cue. Watch his head and arm movements. He *should* look in the direction of his turn; and of course, twisting his steering wheel is a positive tip-off. If an oncoming car ahead starts to veer gradually toward the centerline, it could be the best message you will get, telling you of an upcoming left turn. On the other hand, a faster veer left might be an "out-tracking" movement initiating a *right* turn. Be ready for anything; and make sure you are proceeding with sufficient caution and at a speed sufficiently reduced that you can stop if you have to.

The plainest way I can tell you of the hazard that turning motorists represent is this: *Anytime* a vehicle is in a position where it *can* turn into your path, you'd better be defensively alert for it as a live possibility. Look upon such a driver as you would a man with a gun at your head and his finger on the trigger. This goes for either oncoming vehicles or those in your own traffic flow, headed in your direction. It applies to the possible *left* turn into your path (the most likely according to statistics), by an oncoming vehicle or a cross-traffic vehicle on your right. And it applies to the guy going your way, abreast of you on the left, who can speed up suddenly and cut in front of you because he almost forgot he wants to go right at the next corner.

Ride able to evade

In other words, your hazardous turner could go into action at an intersection, into a driveway, into a shopping center or parking lot, or simply move from another lane into yours. You have to do more than watch for a turn signal that might not be given, or even a tell-tale slowing down. You must travel along a street or highway at such a speed, and in such a lane position, and with such alertness that you can *evade* any motorist who might suddenly turn in front of you.

You must maintain this ability with the knowledge that the turn might very well *not* be a planned move, but a split-second decision. This can and does happen when a daydreaming driver suddenly realizes he has gone past his intended turning point, and decides to do it *right now,* in front of *guess who!*

One of the cyclist fatalities in my state occurred when a 16-year-old 100 cc bike rider was struck by an oncoming motorist who made this type of "spur-of-the-moment" decision. He told officers he suddenly realized he had entered the street in the wrong direction to get to his destination, and made a left turn across the street into a driveway, planning to turn around. The young cyclist, whom the driver "didn't see," was riding about 35 miles per hour right where the abrupt left turn was made. He laid down 23 feet of skid marks, but crashed into the car and was killed.

If avoiding such incidents makes it impossible for you to do 40 in a 40-miles-per-hour zone, make up your mind to it. It's more important to be able to evade this kind of trouble just once in years of riding than it is to go the full speed limit and take chances every day.

Left turners do signal their intentions much of the time; and when I'm across the intersection facing one, I very often wave him on while I wait. Respecting those accident statistics, I just prefer to get the left turner on his way, rather than start across the intersection knowing he might not even see me.

Ask yourself one pertinent question as you ride: Could I safely stop or take evasive action if *that car* suddenly turned in front of me? If you can't give an honest affirmative answer, you are not riding defensively as you must for safety's sake. Remember that it takes about a foot of *reaction* time for each mile-per-hour of your speed—40 feet to react and stop at 20 miles per hour, half of it in reaction time. This means that time and time again you are in a traffic position where your proximity to an oncoming or cross-traffic car makes it difficult or impossible to stop before colliding with an unexpected turner. Be ready to jump a curb if necessary; but your best protection when no median separates you from oncoming traffic is a high level of alertness and cautious speed.

A 14-year-old was killed aboard a 200 cc cycle as he cruised along a county lake road about 50 miles per hour. The bike size, illegal for his age, indicates it was probably borrowed and unfamiliar to him. But it was his failure to be alert for a left turn in front of him that caused his death. In this case, the left turn was made by a 61-year-old man operating a farm tractor on the road. Without signaling, he turned left into his private drive, directly in the path of the boy. After the impact, the cycle went another 15 feet while the rider was ejected 27 feet and killed.

Not all motorcycle fatalities caused by turning vehicles are left-turn situations. If you stick your neck out by riding between a moving lane of traffic and a row of parked cars, worse things can happen than having a door open in your face. An 18-year-old female passenger rode with a cyclist riding in that hazardous location. He thought he could make better time passing a few cars on the right. He did fine past two cars; but the third driver in line, completely unaware of the cycle in his blind spot, made a *right turn* to enter a driveway. In this case, the young man was only slightly injured. But his girlfriend, who wore no helmet, died of massive head injuries. Blame for the accident goes to the operator's action in illegally risking just such a turning hazard by riding to the right of the authorized lane of traffic.

Watch your own turning

Your own turning maneuvers can be hazardous, too, if done improperly. Because of your smaller vehicle size, it can be very tempting to make premature, wide-sweeping left turns that can crowd cross-traffic vehicles dangerously. Instead, go to the intersection center with signal lights flashing, then make your left turn lean directly into your new riding lane. Of course, I *don't recommend* that you make your mid-intersection turn so sharply that you lose your traction security. Keep your speed carefully under control, to prevent going too wide through centrifugal force.

In making right turns, sometimes there is a tendency to lean too close to the curbside. This can result in a footpeg scrape and upset.

Watch lane changers

Lane-changing is a turning maneuver that can also be dangerous to nearby cyclists. What do you do if you are riding on a multi-lane thoroughfare, and a motorist in an adjoining lane takes a fancy to yours, just pulling over as if he owned the world? Not much time for (or point in) horn blowing in this case. *Avoiding* the guy is more sensible. Slow down and let him be, or speed up—whichever is *safer.* That's a quick decision you'll have to make; be *sure* you're right.

Any time you become aware of a hazard to a nearby motorist, get ready for him to take evasive action of his own—*in your direction.* If it doesn't happen that way, well and good; but the chances are that it will, and you need to move accordingly. He probably doesn't even know you're in the vicinity; and even if he does, he'd much rather tangle with you than another motorist. That may not be a nice attitude on his part; but recognizing the reality of it is smart on your part.

As the title of this chapter indicates, your greatest single hazard comes from others turning unexpectedly into your path. It's a maneuver that happens with deadly regularity; don't let it happen to you.

19. Safe Braking

B EING ABLE to stop is one of the basic control operations important to staying alive on a motorcycle. Statistics prove what common sense would tell us. Accident reports reveal that almost half of accident-involved cyclists fail to stop when they should, or maintain proper control of their bikes. This is an accident-causing factor you can do something about or not, as you choose. If you want to stay alive in traffic, *stop* when you're supposed to stop; and keep your cycle under control with the proper alertness and cautious speed at all times.

Stops at signal lights

Stop in any situation where safety dictates it, and always when you are faced with a stop sign or red signal light at an intersection. Less obviously, safe riding requires you to stop on the amber warning light, even if it is legal in your state to start across on amber and finish on the red. You run too great a risk that someone on your right or left will start up early, and you'll have an unpleasant meeting in the center of the intersection.

Stop even though you have the green light if an emergency vehicle is coming through the intersection; if a traffic officer is present and requests you to stop (as in the case of a funeral cortege proceeding through an intersection); or if any obvious hazard overrules the reasonableness of your right-of-way.

Stopping distances

Keep in mind the distance required to stop, and ride accordingly. Chapter 8 contains a chart giving average distances for various speeds; and please don't count on your ability being super rather than average. As a rule of thumb, you can always figure one foot per mile per hour of your speed for *reaction* time alone. That means it will take you 30 feet, riding at 30 miles per hour, just to *begin* applying your brakes. At the legal speed limit of 55 miles per hour, you'll travel more than two-thirds the length of a football field from the time you see a hazard until you have come to a complete stop. That's true for the latest, best brakes; for older models the National Safety Council chart specified an entire 100 yards at only 50 miles per hour.

One thing I would advise is frequent checks on the condition of both the front and rear brakes on your bike. Maintaining them both in a properly adjusted condition guarantees the best possible stopping power for emergencies that will arise.

Be sure to signal

Use your rear brake control pedal to signal your intention to slow down or stop. In order for this to be an effective means of communication to a following driver, don't ride your brakes as a habit; and start slowing early. Form the habit of keeping your foot right above the brake pedal, ready to go into action fast.

Braking sequence

Your front disc brake is the most powerful, and you need to use it cautiously to prevent being thrown, or accidentally turning the throttle when you squeeze the hand lever. But this lever can also be used for signaling purposes if you employ quick, gentle squeezes. Always begin your braking action with the rear (foot pedal) brake.

The front brake must also be used with caution when you are riding on quick-spill surfaces (sand, gravel, water, mud, ice or oil); when your front wheel is turned to one side; or when you are leaning for a turn. Actually, you should do no braking in turns *unless* it becomes necessary to prevent an accident.

Gearing down helps

Many times, when a slowing operation is all that is needed, downshifting will suffice in lieu of braking. Gearing down as you approach an intersection where a stop will be or may be required is a good assist to your braking operation.

Proper braking in normal situations combines the use of both brakes with the gearing-down operation. First, you let off on the throttle and apply the rear brake with your foot pedal. Then as braking begins, you squeeze the hand brake lever to combine the force of both braking systems, and downshift as needed. When your speed drops below 10 miles per hour, you can squeeze the clutch lever. Go into neutral as you come to a smooth stop and put your foot down.

Braking for curves

A 20-year-old riding a 400 cc cycle waited too long before starting to brake for a curve formed by a divided road at the bottom of a sharp downgrade. The downhill run probably helped cause his speed to be too great for the curve, which he failed to make. He went airborne 42 feet, landed alongside an irrigation canal, bounced, flew another 21 feet through the air—all of this still on his bike. At this point he was ejected, and died a few feet beyond the sliding machine. What a price to pay for late braking!

Curves can be deceptive, of course, so what can a rider do who finds out he's still going too fast when he reaches the leaning point? This is the kind of tough question I'd rather not answer. I'd much rather convince you of the life-saving importance of reducing your speed even more than you think is necessary, *before* you go into the curve.

But if you *do* get to the curve at too fast a clip, get in as much braking action as you can before you start to lean. Even then, you may be able to lean a little (during which you do *no* braking), straighten up quickly (during which you apply your brakes hard), then lean into the curve again. How much of this juggling act you can do without going down will depend on your speed, the kind of traction you have, how extreme the curve is, and your coordinating ability.

A 22-year-old rider in a rural area borrowed (his first mistake) a 650 cc and took it out while under the influence of alcohol (his second mistake). While speeding at 60 miles per hour (his third mistake), he rode into a 35-miles-per-hour sharp curve (his *fatal* mistake!) and went out of control. He traveled that way 132 feet, impacted, and came to rest 20 feet farther on, while the cycle bounced another 10 feet.

Emergency braking

When you are riding at high speeds, you will need to plan and execute your stops earlier. This is because the braking action must be gradual rather than abrupt if you are to maintain control. But what about the times when emergency stops become necessary—what braking technique should be followed?

It's dangerous at best; but in such cases sit square in the saddle, shut off all throttle and apply both brakes simultaneously. This has to be done in an upright, straight-steering position, *not* while you are in a turn. Let up on your brakes the very instant you feel a wheel slipping or locking—or if your cycle begins to lean over or go into a sideways skid.

Stops on bad surfaces

Quick-spill surfaces make your front (hand) brake strictly bad news. If your riding surface is *bad*, depend on your *foot* brake. This same rear brake is better to use at slower speeds. But remember to avoid the hand brake when you ride on slippery or skid-prone surfaces such as those covered with sand, gravel, or even a thick layer of dust. On such surfaces, the front wheel is too susceptible to locking up, resulting in a skid. Even when you apply only your rear brake, do it gently on quick-spill surfaces.

Skid control

Controlling skids on a motorcycle is a matter of slowing down without overbraking, applying your brake power while you're upright, and keeping your wheels rolling, with the front wheel *straight*. As a *last resort*, you can try using your well-shod feet to help you straighten up. If *nothing* helps, try to tuck yourself into a ball and land where it looks the safest.

If all this sounds as futile as it may prove to be, you may decide not to get yourself into such a mess; just ride properly in the first place. Braking operations that are dire emergencies are caused by risk-taking, 99 times out of 100.

20. Safe Passing

THE MARYLAND REPORT mentioned often in these pages has *passing* tied for third place in driver skills importance, from a safety standpoint. In all Maryland accidents studied, involving auto/cycle collisions resulting from improper passing, the cyclist was to blame seven times as often as the motorist. This was particularly true of urban accidents, though rural intersection accidents were caused by the cyclist 3-½ times as often as by the motorist.

The rules for motorcycles are almost like those for cars in the matter of passing other vehicles. Your primary concerns will be whether the driver you wish to pass sees you and knows your intention; whether the way is clear, with enough room in which to pass without problems; and what is involved for proper, legal execution of the passing maneuver. These factors will be covered briefly in this chapter.

Try to be seen

Passing requires special care. It will *always* be unsafe to pass another vehicle if its operator doesn't see you; or if he sees you but doesn't know you want to pass. *Never* attempt to pass at a point where it would be illegal. Position yourself in the visible lefthand third of your lane, behind the driver of the car you plan to pass, long enough for him to be aware of your presence before you make your move. Check traffic conditions both to the front and the rear, to make sure you have a safe amount of passing time and space. Then signal your lane change and go ahead. Give him a mild tap on the horn, if you like, to keep him aware of your presence and intentions.

If you are riding behind a truck so large or loaded in such a way that you can't see around, don't risk passing. Bide your time until you get a long, clear stretch; then drop back and pull close enough to the centerline that you gain the necessary visibility to make your passing decision.

Times not to pass

Do not pass under the following circumstances; it will be illegal or too hazardous, or both:

1. On hills or curves.

2. On bridges, viaducts, or overpasses.

3. In tunnels.

4. In no-passing zones (see notes below).

5. At or near intersections, crosswalks or railroad crossings.

6. At any point where your view is obstructed.

7. Any school bus that is loading or unloading passengers, or has its warning light flashing.

8. On a vehicle's right, unless in a legally authorized multilane situation.

As I wrote this chapter, I learned of a case in which a 22-year-old tried to pass in a no-passing zone with a 20-year-old female passenger hanging on, neither of them wearing a helmet. He will never make his 23rd birthday because he died at the scene. She is in critical condition with head and internal injuries. In another case, a couple of teenagers demonstrated this "no-no" when a 15-year-old on a 250 cc tried to pass a car too close to an intersection. The car, driven by a 16-year-old, went into an improper, corner-cutting left turn just at that moment. The cyclist was killed.

Is the passing lane open?

In passing an automobile, do so on the driver's side unless a *legal* righthand passing lane is open *and is safer.* Before you make your move, be *sure* the passing lane is completely open, and that no other vehicle is about to pass you at the same time. Make a head check to the rear; signal your turn and sound your horn; pull into the left lane and pass just as you would if you were driving a car. Don't crowd as you pass; pull ahead far enough for safe clearance (at least until you can see the car being passed in your rear-view); make sure he has not increased his speed to crowd *you*; then signal and pull right again into your original lane. Your passing speed should be moderately brisk but steady until you have gone back to the right; then resume your normal speed.

Passing on the right

Passing on the right is legal on a multilane (four or more) highway if there is sufficient width without obstructions or parked vehicles. Also on a one-direction street or roadway of sufficient width. As far as the law is concerned, it is usually legal to overtake and pass a vehicle on the right if it is in the process of making a left turn. But motorcycle safety calls for extreme caution on this one—too easy to find yourself riding too far right to avoid the turning vehicle; and I have also seen motorists change their minds in midturn and pull back to the right again. That could be very messy.

As you make a legal passing maneuver in the righthand lane, be quick to move up out of the driver's right-side blind spot; and you may want to sound your horn moderately as your pass. This is a tricky option. Hearing your horn without seeing you, the driver might interpret it as a request to *move* right, to permit passing on his left. Or if your horn blast is too loud, it could startle the motorist and cause a swerve in your direction. Do your sounding off carefully, and in advance, while you can still avoid a left-to-right squeeze. If you're not sure the driver is aware of your presence as you pass on his right, just move swiftly alongside and on ahead, giving him a wide berth. Take care not to jeopardize yourself by getting too close to a rutted shoulder or broken curb base.

When you find yourself sandwiched in with a long line of cars, it can be very tempting to pull right and travel to the next intersection between the lane of halted automobiles and the curb. It's especially tempting when you plan to make a right turn at the intersection anyway. *Resist these temptations!* It's not only illegal, it's apt to be suicidal. (You'll consistently find danger and illegality going hand in hand; that's why those laws got on the books.)

Just because all of the cars in the line are standing still with motors idling, that doesn't mean they'll stay that way. There are some motorists who, upon seeing a motorcycle approaching in that curb gap, will deliberately pull right to block him. And just in case you make it to the intersection, there you'll be, illegally shooting the gap between the front car and the curb. If, as will often be the case, this front motorist plans to make a right turn also, you could easily find yourself fighting him for the lead. You'd better know who has the best chance of winning.

If you pass on the right between a driving lane and a line of cars parked at the curb, you multiply your chances for an accident—from another car nudging into the driving lane from a driveway, unnoticed by you because of a parked truck, or from a car door being opened in front of you. Stick with the rules. Your time really isn't so valuable you can afford to take these risks.

Of course, these same hazards will exist when you ride a one-way street next to cars parked on the *left* side of the street, even though you are passing the driving lane automobile on the driver's side. What it boils down to is this: *avoid those tempting gaps* that are illegal or dangerous or both. This includes gaps between a parking lane and a driving lane; between two driving lanes; between a driving lane and a street curb with no parking lane; or on a shoulder between driving lane and bar ditch. Just take time to move as you would in an automobile, because you have the same legal responsibility—and along with it, the vulnerability of a pedestrian.

Group passing

If you ever take part in group riding, passing can be a real problem. It must be done *one at a time,* with each rider rotating up one notch as a pass is completed. As each cycle passes the slow vehicle, he moves up to clear the way and waits for the rest to get back into formation before resuming the agreed trip speed. Oncoming traffic will vary during the passing process. No cyclist in the group should pass until the way is perfectly clear.

When you are being passed

Use great caution when you find yourself *being passed* by another vehicle. Don't compete with its safe passing operation by speeding up as it gets alongside. Instead, help the driver any way you can, perhaps by reducing your speed slightly and pulling to the center of your lane. There is a wind hazard to cyclists being passed, especially when the passing vehicle is a large tractor/trailer rig. Both bow waves and rear suction waves of wind and vacuum can cause you to wobble or lose control, particularly on a light bike.

To illustrate how important it is to pass with care, especially when you are riding with other cyclists, consider the death of one young couple. The 20-year-old male victim was operating a 750 cc, with a 16-year-old girl as his passenger. They were passing a 15-year-old boy riding a 125 cc when he started a left turn. The larger bike with the couple aboard struck the boy on the left side as they passed by. They went out of control, hit the pavement, veered left of the centerline 58 feet into an oncoming car and were both killed. The younger cyclist and the driver of the car were both injured.

21. Safe Turning

TURNING needn't throw you a curve if you pay attention to just a few details.

Proper leaning

You don't "steer" by turning your handlebars to negotiate a curve. As on a bicycle, you just push down with your right hand and use body lean to curve right or make a right turn, and vice versa. As the angle of your cycle changes from upright (90° with surface) to something less (70°, for example), your speed and body action are important control factors in helping to compensate for the weight shift. You'll coordinate these almost automatically if you have a good sense of balance. If you don't, just get right back into a car.

As I have mentioned before, turning leans get to be such fun, there's a danger of wanting to overdo them. After awhile, you may feel you are so good at turns that you can lean another 5° or 10°; and if you get away with that, you think surely you could put it down just a bit more. That's *not* an attitude that leads to survival in traffic—or *out* of traffic. A friend of mine who rode thousands of miles on a cycle before I tried it, decided to quit after a bad cornering spill. There was no contact with any other vehicle; he simply leaned too far at an intersection covered with a thin layer of sand and grit. If the surface had been completely clean, he might have made it with his extreme angle of lean. But the chances are greater that even with the sand, he still would have made it by using a normal leaning angle. *Don't go too far with your cornering lean.* Enough to get the job done is all you want if you're interested in safe riding.

Surfaces *are* especially important on curves, so take each one with an eagle eye to that factor. It's a good habit to check your riding surface as you go; and when taking a curve or a corner, it's even more important.

Proper speed

Your speed is another important factor here. If you find it necessary to lean excessively, you're going *too fast* for turning safety. Let up a little on the throttle—enough to return to a safe lean. My very first accident was due to excessive throttle during a left-turn operation. I panicked and failed to let up on the throttle sufficiently as I turned.

Letting up on the throttle reduces both your speed and your turning arc. Too much throttle will broaden your turning arc, and the centrifugal force will put you into oncoming traffic or a curb. So the rule becomes simple: *let up* on your throttle to *reduce* your turning arc; give it *more* throttle to *broaden* your turning arc. Push down on the handle grip in the direction of your turn, and lean with your body. Make this cycle-to-surface angle of lean enough to negotiate the curve or corner, and no more. Practice in a traffic-free parking lot to get the hang of right and left turns, U-turns and complete circles with proper amount of lean.

Slowing for a turn can be accomplished by downshifting, braking or both. Begin early, while you are still on a straight run. If you wait until you are in the middle of your turn to use your brakes, the odds in favor of a skid increase fantastically. This is because your traction decreases in a turning maneuver; and you need maximum traction for braking. As you complete your turn, pick up speed to put you back on a straight-line run.

Too much speed going into a turn is a real killer for cyclists. A 21-year-old on a 750 cc cycle went into a sharp curve on the inside of two southbound lanes at 60 miles per hour, and it was simply too fast for control. His speed carried him into a ¾-ton truck in the outside lane and he died at the scene.

When you mix with fast traffic, you will find yourself having to move into curves faster than you would normally prefer. Remember to turn more gradually at high speeds, but be sure to lean into the turn enough that you don't run off on the outside of the curve. Keep your body at the same angle as your bike. Lean *enough*, not *too much*. Keep your eyes ahead of you, where you want to move through the curve. Accelerate as you leave the curve and go into the straightaway.

What to do when going into a curve too fast was covered in Chapter 19; but the real answer is *not* to go into a curve too fast. If the flow of traffic is too fast for safety as you approach a curve, let the speed demons on four wheels behind you know you are *not* going into the curve at such speeds. It's much better to deal with tailgating at this point than it will be when you get into the curve. If one of these motorists gets impatient and swishes around you, be sure to give him as much passing room as possible. Also, be ready for the possible squeeze play emergency he could generate.

By the numbers

A typical sequence of actions in a turning maneuver would go like this:

1. Determine well in advance *where* you want to turn. Sudden, last-minute turns are almost always hazardous in their execution.

2. *Signal* your intentions.

3. Swivel your neck for a careful head check to see where other vehicles are and how fast they are going. This is essential to safe lane-changing and turns. In turning right, watch out for a car on your left about to make the same move. You could be forced into the curb.

4. Get into the correct turning lane as quickly as possible.

5. Slow down to a safe turning speed *before* you reach the intersection or curve. Don't try braking or gearing actions while you execute the turn. Don't slow so much that you lose control.

6. Keeping your feet on the pegs, make your turn correctly as has been discussed, and finish in the proper lane. (If you actually reach the intersection in an improper lane, go on to

the next turning intersection and make your move from the proper lane.)

7. Never overtake another vehicle in a curve.

8. Never make a turn unless it is both *legal* and *safe*.

How you can miss a curve

Failing to negotiate a curve is a high fatality factor for cyclists. Basically there are only three causes for the problem:

1. Failure to see the curve soon enough—too much speed or too little attention.

2. Getting into the turn at an excessive speed—applying brakes too hard and fast. This is often caused by not "Riding Ahead."

3. Trying to make the curve without slowing, or without slowing enough—uncontrolled centrifugal force.

Signals save lives

Your pre-turn slowing and signaling must both be done well ahead of your turning point; so the two should be coordinated. Your signal comes first, whether by hand or by using your electric turn signals. Hand signals must be practiced, because one-handed operation gives you less control. I rely on my signal lights, which are more visible than hand signals, especially when it is cloudy, foggy, rainy, or when you ride at night. Don't take it for granted that you are safe because you signal. This action only serves to communicate with other vehicle operators around you. Make a cautious head check before going ahead with your turn. *After* completing a turn, be sure to cancel your electric turn indicators.

Failing to signal is a carelessness indulged in by more and more motorists; but it is a luxury you simply can't afford if you want to stay alive on a motorcycle. One fatal accident took place when a 13-year-old operating a 100 cc bike turned off of a U.S. highway onto a county road at 40 miles per hour. He gave no signal for the turn; and both he and his 15-year-old brother riding as a passenger were killed by an overtaking semi-trailer/tractor rig. The tractor was making 55 miles per hour, and the boy may not have realized how fast he would be overtaken. But a proper turn signal would have given the trucker the warning he needed. *Signaling can save your life!*

Use your eyes well

Watching out for other vehicles turning into your path is as important as proper signaling and turning on your part. Yield to them, even when you have the right-of-way.

Proper use of your mirrors before turning is good; but turning your head for a positive look in changing lanes or making turns is even better. After all, *you* have a blind spot to left and right also, just as motorists have.

Avoid wide-arc turning

Just as you must reduce your speed before reaching your turning point, there is another side of the coin: don't begin a left-turn maneuver *until* you reach that point. Go to the center of the intersection, then make a well-controlled, unhesitating left turn. Slipping the clutch helps your coordination during these comparatively tight turns. Fast, wide-arc turning is out; too many unexpected hazards can arise from cross-traffic vehicles or pedestrians.

Right turns

In making a right turn in brisk traffic, be sure the way is clear and you're in the right lane, then get on with it. Slowing down too much here can put you into the middle of a squeeze play. If there are pedestrians, plan your timing before you start your turn, even if you have to slow the traffic behind you to a standstill.

U-turn hazards

U-turns are legal in some locations, though extra caution is always advisable in making them. Some U-turns are completely beyond reason. An example is the one attempted at night in a metropolis by a 22-year-old riding a 750 cc. He was being followed by a 2-ton truck.

What the trucker thought he saw was a cyclist pulling off to the righthand edge of the street to make a stop. He thought the cycle rider wanted him to go on past, and that's what he proceeded to do.

What the biker planned to do was to pull to the right in an out-tracking move, then cut back to the left in an illegal U-turn. The two tangled (both the truck driver and the bike rider were under the influence of alcohol), and you know who came out unhurt. The cyclist lost a leg and died a short time later in the hospital.

Remember that U-turns are the equivalent of two consecutive right or left turns. This means there is twice the opportunity for you to lose your balance by too much lean, or to run off at the outside of the long curve.

22. Give Hazards a Wide Berth

REAR-END collisions constitute one of the leading motorcycle safety problems. In both the Maryland study and a recent highway patrol report from my state, this "following too close" factor ranked fourth among the various causes. While tailgating is only one of a number of ways you can get too close to a traffic hazard, it deserves special mention. According to the Motorcycle Safety Foundation summary report, a fourth of all motorcycle/other vehicle accidents are rear-end collisions; and in most cases it is the motorcycle striking the rear end of the other vehicle. Most often, these collisions *do not* happen in an intersection; and this is true whether the cyclist or the motorist is at fault.

Following too close means just what it says; you are riding too close to an accident about to happen. The accident will involve *you*; so if you think about it, that's a pretty dumb way to ride a cycle. When street traffic is moving moderately, keep two or three car lengths between you and the motorist ahead. When you're going 35 or 40 miles per hour, broaden the gap even more; but try not to encourage followers to move in front of you, defeating your purpose. (This advice doesn't mean to *contest* with following vehicles for the space ahead of you; just try to arrive at a "happy medium" safe distance that will give you adequate reaction and stopping time for emergencies and yet not be too inviting for vehicles behind you.) You'll find it a lot harder to become an accident statistic if you give yourself maximum reaction time to potential emergencies; and that is what street space ahead of you represents.

State laws are usually nonspecific in the matter of following distances considered safe and legal. Generally the language is something like this:

"A driver of a motor vehicle shall not follow another vehicle more closely than is reasonable and prudent, having due regard for speed, traffic and conditions of the roadway."

This leaves the matter to the judgment of the driver—and the judgment of officers and traffic court judges in the event of an accident. Both your health and your wallet will remain in better shape if you play it safe. Use the stopping distances chart as a guide, if you like, leaving at least 40 feet between you and the car in front of you if you are both going 20 miles per hour, and so on. Memorize the chart if it will help; but make it more than a mental exercise. Stay far enough behind to give you safe maneuvering and stopping room if the vehicle ahead should stop. And stay far enough behind a large truck to avoid being caught in the suction it creates on the highway.

One method of establishing a safe following distance without having to concentrate on the number of feet or car spaces between you and the vehicle ahead, is known as the "Two-Second Count" method. In operation, you simply give a slow two-count from the time the vehicle in front of you passes a given object (telephone pole, parked car, etc.), and make sure *you* don't pass the same object until your count is complete. A *slow* two-count, by the way, is made by saying to yourself "one thousand *one*; one thousand *two*." I don't know any reason why an unhurried five-count (omitting the "one thousand") wouldn't accomplish the same thing if you prefer. At least one authority recommends a three-second count. I find in actually timing my slow two-count (or the five-count omitting the "one thousand") that three seconds does elapse.

The nice thing about this counting technique is that as your riding speed varies, the safe distance automatically varies in the same ratio. At a faster speed, for example, you need greater separation—and the counting time automatically gives you more distance between yourself and the vehicle ahead. The other method (estimating distance by car lengths or feet) becomes more difficult as you increase your speed.

Watch for turns

There are times when you can get involved in a rear-end accident even if you're not following very close. A 20-year-old riding a 350 cc bike was traveling at 45 miles per hour behind a pickup truck. He wasn't tailgating; but neither was he ready for the pickup driver to turn into a driveway without signaling. He collided with the pickup, then skidded 23 feet into another truck in oncoming traffic. He was dead on arrival at the hospital. My contention is that in spite of the non-signal turn for which the pickup driver was cited, the young man would be alive if he had been riding at least 150 feet behind, as the 45 miles per hour speed requires for safety. Getting to his intended destination 100 feet sooner, by riding only 50 feet behind the pickup, just wasn't worth the risk he took.

Watch for sudden stops

There are also times when you can be traveling quite slow and still tangle with a vehicle in a rear-end collision. I was starting slowly up from a traffic light stop when I proved this point. An elderly lady motorist ahead of me started a left turn on a green arrow signal, and I followed. When she began to wonder if a motorist facing us from across the intersection had failed to see the left-turn signal as he began inching forward, she tromped on her brake pedal and stopped in my face.

Both of these examples should tell you that without a good crystal ball to tell you when and how traffic circumstances are going to change suddenly, you need to give every hazard a wide berth.

Visibility problem

When you fail to put enough distance ahead of you, some of your visibility is automatically impaired. The car or truck you're following will keep you from being able to scan the surface of your roadway for potholes or other hazards; and they may obscure a hazard that is developing ahead from oncoming vehicles.

Besides the sudden-stop hazard of the vehicle in front of you, keep in mind that a four-wheeler can easily straddle and pass over an object in the street big enough to put you down quickly should you hit it. The very least you need to protect yourself against such obstacles is enough time after spotting it to engage it with the least risk; and it would be much better if you had time to dodge it altogether. Again, the only way you can have this much maneuvering time is to maintain a safe distance between your cycle and the vehicle ahead.

Watch for out-track moves

It has been mentioned that the out-tracking maneuver can be a legitimate move for cyclists making a sharp corner. It can also be an unnecessary and deceiving move by a motorist driving just ahead of you. But it will only be cause for concern if you are following too close behind, and mistake an initial move to the right to indicate a right turn, or vice versa, only to have the driver whip back in the other direction unexpectedly and wind up right in your lap. The simple solution is just to give every motorist plenty of room to do his thing (even when it's weird or illegal) without involving you.

Appraise drivers

As you approach another vehicle from the rear, it pays to make an appraisal of the driver's ability and mood. If he is a stable person driving legally and cautiously, you can afford to ride closer to him than would be the case if he appears to be erratic or intoxicated.

With experience you will be able to make such decisions. In any event, keep that safe stopping distance in mind; even the best driver can be confronted with a sudden emergency ahead without your knowledge until his brakes flash.

Emergency vehicles

Ride alert to any emergency vehicles that might appear on the scene, and give them the wide berth that is dictated not only by safety considerations, but by the law. Remember the special privileges school buses are accorded; be particularly cautious as you follow one.

How to keep your distance

Depending on the situation, your safe distance can be maintained by slowing down, increasing your speed, moving to one side, sounding your horn or flashing your brake lights in warning. Because you and your bike take up less space than other vehicles, you can minimize potential dangers from either side by moving laterally within your traffic lane. Sometimes a combination of speed change and lateral move will maximize your safety.

Making your lateral move decisions is a matter of good sense and experience. If you approach an intersection with a cross-traffic vehicle at both your right and left, riding in the left third of your lane will give you the maximum distance from both. Suppose you are riding in the passing lane of a four-lane street with no median, and an oncoming truck pulls into the lane to your left in a passing move. What do you do to achieve the safest position? If the lane to your right is open, you can move into the right third of that lane. If not, move to the *center* of the lane you are occupying. This will put you halfway between the oncoming truck and the right-lane vehicle. You will want to avoid the center-lane position when possible, for reasons we have mentioned before; but it is generally safer for temporary periods than a close proximity to adjacent vehicles.

In making hazard-minimizing moves like these, always decide where the greatest potential danger lies, and establish your safe distance accordingly. "Ride Ahead" mentally, in order to avoid getting yourself into squeeze plays. The earlier you can identify where and how trouble might arise, the more options you have to maintain your safe separation from other vehicles in the traffic pattern.

Safe passing room

Give plenty of room to a vehicle you are passing. Too many cyclists think the name of this game is to zoom in close to the rear of a car, swoop suddenly to the left and ahead, then cut in close to the front of the car being passed, speeding ahead with a deafening roar. Safe passing calls for establishing your position at a safe following distance in the left third of the lane, so the driver is aware of your presence. Then move left into the passing lane, again taking up a left-third position and moving ahead with a steady throttle, *not* at an excessive speed. Wait until your cycle is far enough ahead that the car being passed is visible in your rear-view mirror, then move back into the right lane. If there is oncoming traffic as you pass, center your cycle in the passing lane; or if traffic conditions permit, wait until there is no oncoming vehicle next to the centerline before making your passing move.

Increase for bad weather

When the weather turns bad, increase the distance between you and hazards. The reason is obvious: you can't *see* as well and you can't *stop* as well under rainy, cloudy or foggy conditions. Even in good weather, if you find the sun in your eyes, or if you are riding in a spot where it is glaring off another vehicle and giving you vision problems, back off until the problem is corrected. *Do not* move laterally in your lane to correct the glare if you are already riding in the safest lane position. Night riding is another time to widen the safe distance gap, to give you more reaction and maneuvering time for emergencies.

Pets and bicycles

When pets appear in the roadway ahead of you, try to stay clear of them if possible; they're either unpredictable, or predictable aggressors. Reduce your speed and gear down; if they haven't cleared by the time you reach them, speed up and leave them—but not in a risky manner.

Give bicycle riders the same courtesy and wide-berth separation you would in the case of powered vehicles. They can be just as great a hazard as a car or truck.

On Highway 66 an 18-year-old rider on a 750 cc rear-ended an 11-year-old on a bicycle. No question about the risk the bicyclist was taking on the highway; but it was a clear day on a dry surface when he lost his life in this accident. The scene was on a downgrade, and it is possible that the motorcyclist (who was injured in the accident) didn't realize how fast he was closing behind the bicycle. Apparently, however, the safe distance rule was not observed.

Stationary objects

Remember to give *stationary objects* a wide berth as well as moving vehicles. You know they aren't going anywhere; so it will be clear where the blame belongs if you run into anything that can't defend itself. A 22-year-old riding a 350 cc bike rode too close to a local bridge abutment and lost his life in the accident. He struck the bridge at 45 miles per hour, and was ejected into a creek bed.

Being crowded

We've been considering primarily the problems you might create for yourself as a rider following too close, or failing to give enough lateral separation between you and potential hazards. But what of the tailgater who makes you a target? You can communicate with him by flashing your brake light (quick, easy hand squeezes are all that are required)—and I have found this very effective. At other times, you may find it necessary to turn in your saddle and vigorously *wave him back*, or wave him *around* you, as you prefer. The main thing is to let him know, in eyeball-to-eyeball fashion, that he is an immediate hazard to you and you want him to "bug off."

I have seen a car filled with people actually force a motorcycle rider off an expressway by moving to within inches of his tail light at high speed. He saved himself only by taking an exit ramp that luckily was at hand. I'll never know why the driver of the car pulled this stunt; but if it happens to you, be smart enough to get out of the way just as this rider did; use the shoulder if no exit is handy. If you're not too "shook," get the license number and *prosecute*. You have as much legal right to the use of our streets and highways as any motorist.

Crowding and tailgating are two different things. Tailgating, or following too close, is one form of crowding; but one vehicle can crowd another from other directions than the rear, and *do*. It is this practice in which the motorist has been found frequently guilty. In the Maryland report, he crowded the cyclist eleven times as often as the reverse was true. All the more reason to *give him a wide berth*, using lateral separation and safe distance procedures for all they're worth. Being crowded by a bully with four wheels and wraparound steel is something we can do without.

When you are being crowded, move laterally to achieve a safer separation. If there is no place to escape that way, change your speed and *then* move right or left to shake the offender. But in each case, be sure to defend yourself promptly, by the best means available. *Don't* try to bluff the guy out or insist he give you your right-of-way at the expense of a collision. In that event, you can't possibly win.

23. Overtakers and Undertakers

IF MY title for this chapter seems too "cute" for such a serious subject, I apologize. But the unfortunate truth is, some overtakers do bring on the undertakers for motorcycle riders who have their defenses down. It pays to keep as aware as you possibly can about what is going on behind you. If potential hazards would only *stay* behind you, well and good; but they can come on strong if you're not 100% defensively alert.

When you're standing

When you're stopped at an intersection waiting for a traffic light to change, keep checking your rear-view mirrors to be sure some nut isn't bearing down on you at an uncomfortable overtaking speed. It *might* be someone who "doesn't see" you; or their perspective could be off so badly they could bump you before they realize they're that close. It could even be a parent trying to correct a small child and drive at the same time, or any number of other situations where distraction could lead to your destruction. In any of these cases, I would flash that bright red brake light for all it's worth. If no slowdown is forthcoming, get out of his way! The driver may just be testing your nerves and chuckling; but if he happens to be a drunken idiot, you could wind up dead. Don't risk it.

Motorists assume too much

Some motorists behind you will try to read your mind, on the basis of what they might do in your situation while driving a car. It's entirely possible to be rear-ended or forced into a busy intersection by some joker who decides you can't *possibly* stop in time for a fast-changing signal light. He expects you to head right on into the intersection during the last amber flicker, pushing across as the red comes on. After all, that's what *he* would do; how is he to know you have both the capability of stopping and the intent as well? So there you both are: you trying to be a law-abiding cycle rider by stopping with magnificent swiftness; and "Doubting Thomas" gliding right on up to the raw edge of the intersection (including *your* space) because he is convinced in his own mind you won't even *try* to stop so quickly. You can see the problem; just be sure you're ready for it. This calls for "expecting the unexpected"—dealt with in more detail in the final chapter.

Watch your rear-views

Knowing at all times what your rear-view mirrors can tell you is vital—while you're moving, as well as when you are stopped at intersections. One terrible cycle accident wiped out *two* unhelmeted 14-year-olds, each riding a small bike and making less than 5 miles per hour as they rode together on a county road. They were killed when a 16-year-old with a restricted driver's license overtook them at a speed of 80 miles per hour! He did manage to lay down 146 feet of skid marks before broadsiding one cyclist attempting a U-turn. Then after another 37 feet he struck the second cycle, knocking it 356 feet and ejecting the rider to his death. Both the car and the first cycle traveled another 124 feet and hit a ditch. The cycle went another 21 feet and the rider was thrown 9 feet farther on; he was dead at the scene. The car continued another 38 feet along the ditch, overturned, and threw a passenger out. Both occupants of the car were injured. The cyclists must have heard the speeding car approaching. Harking back to the theme of Chapter 1, I have to say 14-year-olds are not safe on motorcycles on a public roadway. They should have "split" when they heard this menace coming.

When you know danger is on its way, don't dilly-dally. He who rides and runs away will live to ride another day. If a "pusher" doesn't respond quickly to your "Get Back" warning with brake light or hand signal, it's much safer to get out of his way in the best possible direction, and let him annoy a fellow four-wheeler. And if a speeder bears down on you from the rear at anything even approaching 80 miles per hour, don't bother to signal; just get lost.

More overtaker hazards

Keep in mind that when your multilane highway narrows, when cars merge into your lane from a junction or expressway entrance ramp, and when you are approaching construction or accident scenes, the vehicles behind you are more apt to become hazards. Keep well aware of the scene in your rear-views, and be ready to change your speed, your lane position, or from one lane to another to avoid the danger of being overtaken.

When trouble is ahead

If trouble arises *ahead*, putting you into a squeeze as you hit the brakes while another vehicle is overtaking you, there are only two basic choices to make. You can go ahead and move closer to the car ahead, giving the overtaker more time to stop; or you can head for the shoulder. If you wait *too* long to make this latter decision, even the shoulder might not be safe; the overtaker might not stop at all until he plows into the car ahead, with you only a few feet away at the side. In your early cycling years, just remember it's much smarter to be and look overly cautious than to be and look overly dead.

When your safe zone shrinks

You may recall I quoted statistics showing that more than 70% of the rear-end collisions between cycles and other vehicles happen when the cyclist runs into the motorist. To avoid this, be very alert in following. Watch for the brake light, and get your foot on your own brake pedal quickly. If you notice the safe distance ahead beginning to shrink, slow immediately and get ready for anything. Stopped or standing vehicles ahead could spell trouble. Again, reduce your speed and be alert. As you ride, try to *anticipate* problems that could develop for the driver or drivers ahead. Their problems can quickly become *your* problems.

If your cycle stalls

Should *your* machine stall, don't pose a hazard to approaching vehicles; it will only endanger you even more. A 25-year-old riding a 360 cc cycle had engine failure while riding on the highway at night. He was still in the roadway when he was struck and killed by a big car driven by a man who was "under the influence." When you stop on a road or street, move off to safety *immediately.*

24. Safe Entering/Exiting

HOW YOU and other vehicles nearby enter and exit from the traffic flow has a lot to do with your staying alive on a motorcycle. Beginning right where you live, as you prepare to enter the street, defensive alertness must be your watchword. As a matter of fact, driveways of various kinds constitute a major hazard potential. The National Safety Council reports a California study showing that in two-vehicle non-intersection accidents, motorcycle riders are much more accident-prone if either vehicle is entering or leaving a driveway or alley.

Entering your street

At home, arrange your parking space such that you face the street as you enter it. If that space is too limited for a turnaround, back your cycle into place when you park. As you enter the street, check both directions for traffic and wait until there is plenty of clear space before taking off. If you park some distance back from the street, go to the curb line and check traffic carefully before getting underway.

When you have to ride down an *elevated* driveway into a street lined with parked cars, remain at the *top* until you have an all-clear street situation. If you wait till you get to street level to check the traffic flow, all those parked cars interfere with your view. When you see the all-clear condition, ride down, enter the lane you plan to use, and immediately re-check the traffic situation, using your rear-view mirrors.

Watch driveway traffic

As you ride along residential areas, bear in mind that most single-residence automobiles will be *backed* out of the driveway. It's almost impossible for drivers to see you in this operation; so you must check every driveway visually as you go. I regularly ride through one lovely residential area where the street winds in a series of right and left curves. It's enjoyable; but I keep a wary eye glued on each driveway. Some of them are partially hidden by hedges; all are angled to the street in such a way that I have to ride doubly alert. Open alleyways, both in residential and commercial sections, are also places to watch carefully.

As you pass by driveways, hold your left-third position in your half-street-width lane even though there is no centerline stripe. This gives you the maximum opportunity to detect and avoid cars, bicycles, etc. entering the street on your right.

When motorists enter or leave a driveway, even though they know you are approaching, it's very easy for them to underestimate your speed—or give you credit for being able to stop faster than you can. Underestimating the speed of a 23-year-old aboard a 750 cc cycle was very understandable in the case of a motorist trying to enter his private drive from a highway. Understandable because the cyclist, who had been drinking, was eating up space at the rate of 80 to 100 miles per hour—suicide speeds even for a sober biker. The motorist didn't get his left turn completed before the motorcycle struck his left rear in a fatal impact.

View obstructions at entering points apply both ways—when a motorist is backing out of a hidden drive ahead of you, and when you are wheeling out of a driveway unseen by an approaching motorist. Double alertness is the answer in both cases. An 11-year-old boy was leaving a private drive at a point where his view of the county road was obscured by weeds. He was struck broadside by a car, thrown on top of it, carried there for 98 feet, then thrown off. He suffered serious head and leg injuries.

Does your own driveway have traffic-obscuring shrubbery or trees? *Any time* you can't see where you want to go on a cycle, proceed at a crawl pace until you *can* see, before entering a stream of traffic. I wish our stop signs carried the same message the old railroad crossing signs had: not only STOP, but LOOK and LISTEN as well. If the 11-year-old had done this, he could have saved his life. He had no legal right, of course, to go onto the county road on a motorcycle in the first place; but a licensed adult can make the same mistake he did, through carelessness.

Be alert at intersections

Of course, driveways are but a part of the entering/exiting hazards picture. Intersections make up another part of the problem. Local laws generally say that in the absence of traffic signs or signals, a driver on the left must yield to the driver on his right. A better safety rule for motorcycle riders is: *always* give a motorist the right-of-way at an open intersection, if he will take it. Usually they will with little or no encouragement. As for state and federal highways, you are expected to be just this generous at open intersections. "Yield to any approaching traffic and proceed only when it is safe to do so," is the language quoted by our Highway Patrol.

A vehicle that has already entered the intersection has the legal right-of-way over one which has not yet entered. This is true *regardless* of the nature of the intersection. At four-way stop intersections, when two or more vehicles arrive simultaneously, the "driver on the right" principle of right-of-way prevails.

Again at intersections, view obstruction can be a real danger, particularly in rural areas where weeds become overgrown. A couple of years back, a 15-year-old riding a 50 cc minibike entered onto a highway from a side road that was obscured from cross-traffic by trees and high grass. He was hit by a pickup going 50 miles per hour. The pickup skidded 67 feet before and 106 feet after the impact. The cycle rider was ejected, and died at the scene. Whether you can't see or can't *be* seen, the result can be just as fatal. In either case, don't enter the traffic stream until you use a crawl pace to position yourself to see *and* be seen, and wait for a clear opening.

Good, clear intersections won't help if you ignore such simple precautions as stopping at a sign or signal before proceeding. A 19-year-old and his 21-year-old passenger on a 450 cc entered a U.S. highway from one of our state parks without stopping at the sign. As a result, they were struck by a fuel tank truck that happened to be speeding nearly 55 miles per hour in a 30-miles-per-hour reduced-speed zone next to the intersection. The tanker put down 65 feet of skid marks before the impact and 361 feet afterwards, dragging the cycle underneath. Sparks from the cycle being scraped along the highway set both vehicles on fire. Meanwhile the operator was knocked 214 feet from the point of impact, the passenger was thrown off onto the highway, and both were killed.

Chapter 9 stressed obeying the law. You can never enter an intersection legally or safely if you enter it without that careful STOP/LOOK/LISTEN routine. *Make* it "routine," and save your life.

Enter/exit ramps

The situation is different when you are entering or leaving a highway from an access ramp. As nearly as possible commensurate with safety, you should enter and merge smoothly into the traffic stream at a speed approximately that of vehicles already on the highway. To do this, you must use the acceleration lane to achieve this speed. *Do not* go in at a sharp angle after clearing the ramp; and don't let yourself be pushed into the traffic flow by an entering tailgater. If it isn't safe, give him the definite signal that you are hanging tough, and wait until there is a clear spot before moving onto the highway. In exiting, get in the proper lane and signal well in advance and very clearly; use the deceleration lane to its fullest, and go into the exit ramp at or below the recommended exit speed. Same advice as above for tailgaters exiting behind you.

While we're on this subject of expressways and highways where above-limit speeds are par for the course, let me warn you that you automatically subject yourself to increased danger in these places. The fast-moving vehicles are driven by frustrated folk, each of whom knows he could be another Mario Andretti if given half a chance. They don't appreciate motorcycles invading their "track." They are not even as careful or courteous as are the drivers in routine city street traffic (and we've already discussed *their* behavior as being reckless and discourteous far too often). You may be mixing with sleepy, slow-reacting drivers who have been on the highway too long without a break.

All of this adds up to higher odds for an accident, and those odds
are heavy enough anytime. If you don't *have* to travel by these high-
speed arteries, don't take the extra risk; the time you save isn't worth
it. If you like to take the crosstown expressway because you can
achieve extra speed legally, and enjoy the "racetrack feeling" you get
there, you've already identified yourself as an accident looking for a
place to happen. If you are a street bike rider, ride the streets and live
longer. Take to the highways in the comfort and greater safety of an
automobile.

If you *do* ride the expressway, keep a constant watch on those entering ramps. If you see you are about to "come out even" with a guy
preparing to enter your lane, check to see if you can accommodate
him *safely* with a lane change. Use the head-check, don't just look at
your rear-views. If the way just isn't clear for you to move left and let
him come in, it's just one more time when air horns will repay their
investment. For what it's worth, that entering vehicle *is* legally
obliged to slow or stop before merging if his entrance would place
you in a hazardous position. Your air horns (in a series of quick, hard
blasts) can at least serve as a forceful caution, letting the motorist
know your intentions are to proceed past the ramp entrance in your
present lane.

Head-check rule

By the way, my own simplified rule about head-checks versus mirror-
checks is this: when *leaving* a traffic stream in an exiting maneuver,
the mirror-check should suffice. It will, that is, if you have been diligent in keeping track of overtaking traffic all along. But when you are
preparing to *enter* a fast-moving stream of traffic, or merge with another at some form of "Y" junction, give it a full head-check. Swivel
your neck as much as you need, to get a clear picture of all the surrounding traffic. Cyclists have blind spots, too.

About parking places

Just a word about entering and leaving parking places. You naturally
have an advantage over motorists when it comes to entering a parallel parking space at curbside. The usual procedure for the motorist is

to pull alongside the car in front of the vacant space, and back in. If this tempts you to slip easily into the same space before he can back in, forget the temptation. We need all the good relations we can have with motorists; and places to park are a good deal easier to come by for you than for motorists. When you *do* park, position your bike in the center of the space to give as much maneuvering room as possible fore and aft, for drivers of autos. Be sure your kickstand is secure.

In leaving a parking space, signal your intentions just as you were taught to do (but promptly forgot about) when driving a car. If you parked on a level spot, your only concern is avoiding potential conflict with traffic when you pull out into the street. If you are between parked cars, you can't be seen by approaching motorists. If you have parked on an incline, you have the added problem of more difficult balance as you leave the space. I've seen a few beginners swagger up to their parked machine, unlock the fork, insert key in ignition and start up—then kick up the kickstand only to have the inclined weight of the cycle come around in an arc, toppling the whole thing before the rider could take control.

So, if you are parked on an incline, get properly mounted and grip the hand brake before you kick up the stand. If you're leaving on an upgrade, give it enough throttle to provide the extra thrust required. If you leave headed downhill, move quickly out of first into second gear, then let traffic conditions tell you whether to toe on up or ride in second to the next intersection. By all means, *know* the surrounding traffic conditions before you pull away from *any* parking space. The Maryland study found that non-intersection failure-to-yield accidents were caused by vehicles improperly leaving a parking space more often than any other reason.

To repeat what is worth remembering: a major hazard of entering/exiting—whether driveways, intersections, traffic circles, alleys, expressways or highways are involved—is the factor of not being able to *see* or *be seen*. If you fail to observe a stop sign or signal light before entering an intersection or highway, you put yourself into danger before you can be aware of it—and before others can be aware of you. The cyclist has an inherent advantage over the motorist in his ability to see what's going on around him. Don't give up this advantage through default by entering or exiting in a careless or reckless manner.

25. Riding Safely on Hills

KNOWING how to take upgrades and downgrades properly is important for more reasons than just avoiding embarrassment. Stalling on a climb can put you in danger from following traffic. Topping the crown of a hill too fast or in the wrong position can put you into confrontation with an unseen hazard too late for successful evasive action.

There is a best lane

Whether you are going up a hill or down, your first safety task is selecting the lane position that's best, and shifting down into a gear that will give you maximum control. The lane-and-position choice will depend on exactly where you can have the best separation from other vehicles and (if uphill-bound) possible unseen hazards beyond the crest. Your downshifting must take place before you begin to climb or descend.

Uphill riding

In riding up a hill, you need to maintain traction, sufficient momentum and good wheel-to-surface contact. After deciding on your safest lane and/or position within the lane, go into it with positive throttle action and with your body leaning forward in the saddle to give proper weight distribution. The greater the incline, the farther you will lean forward; experience will be your teacher.

You will, of course, lose speed in relation to the grade angle, quality of surface traction and proximity to any roadway obstacles you encounter. You must adjust throttle accordingly, being most intent on avoiding motor stall. Practice on easy hills first, and intentionally let your speed decrease until you recognize the sound and feel of an imminent stall. Do this when no traffic is present; and beware of applying too much throttle too fast in preventing the stall. Otherwise you'll be introduced to the "thrill" of a wheelie in the worst possible place to cope with one.

If you start up a hill in first gear and start to stall out, you have no motor power to prevent it. It's best just to avoid climbing any hill you can't take in second gear without too much loss of speed. Your hill-climbing ability will depend to a great degree on the power of your particular street cycle. If it won't pull them, stay away from them.

If you *do* stall on a steep hill, you need to be able to control, reposition and restart your cycle in a minimum of space and time. If practice in a safe location fails to give you this ability, either avoid hills or consider switching to a machine that is easier-handling, or one that won't stall out on upgrades.

When you climb a hill with a stop sign or signal at the top, you will have to stop much of the time. If your street bike is light enough, it's no problem to hold it steady by planting your toes solid, keeping your knees well forward of your feet, and gripping your hand brake firmly. When you go from neutral into first gear for your take-off, shift your weight to the nongearing foot and move out quickly, but not with a jerk. If your cycle weight/size is too much for you to handle in these hilltop situations, stay off the hills or get a different bike—same as for the stalling problem. *Don't* depend on holding this steep position by remaining in gear and slipping your clutch in a series of false start-ups.

Unsafe cresting

Being able to negotiate a hill without stalling, and always topping a rise safely are two different matters. Not knowing what's on "the other side of the mountain," the motorcycle rider can at least move from the left-third lane position to the right third, and reduce speed in preparation for a quick evasive maneuver that could be needed.

One 22-year-old rider was making 55 miles per hour at night when he topped a hill to find a car *parked facing him*, in his own lane. The driver of the car and three passengers were standing alongside it when the cycle came over the hill. The rider hit his brakes, skidded 49 feet and slid broadside into the car.

After his death it was determined that the cyclist had been drinking; but under his speed and visibility conditions the result would have been the same had he been a teetotaler. The car was illegally parked, creating a senseless hazard. But it could just as easily have been a stray cow in the road, or a large, dead dog that had been stuck minutes earlier. It was the cyclist's speed and lack of alertness for the possibility of hazards hidden from his sight by the hill that kept him from avoiding the accident. *Anytime, anywhere* it is difficult or impossible to see for a safe distance in *all* directions—is the time and place to *reduce* your *speed* and *increase* your *alertness*. Topping a hill at night is certainly such a time and place.

If you have already downshifted before climbing a hill, you will be in a low gear that gives you quick power to avoid such problems as an oncoming driver *passing* on the hilltop, or swerving across the centerline. Even if your bike has the capability of negotiating the hill in its top gear, shifting down is still a good precautionary measure for this very reason.

Topping a hill at high speed is never smart, particularly if you are not familiar with the way the roadway continues on the other side. Two riders on a big cycle were making 55 miles per hour in a 25 miles-per-hour residential zone when they topped an unfamiliar hill. They couldn't handle the sharp right turn on the immediate far side of the hill, and went over a guard rail and fence. That would have been trouble enough; but beyond the fence was a bluff that ran along an expressway below. They fell to their deaths onto railway tracks in the median of that expressway.

Riding down a hill

In riding downgrade, you still need to maintain traction and good wheel-to-surface contact. Gear down for downhill runs, just as you do in a car when the hill is quite steep. Losing speed is no problem here; gaining *too much* momentum *is*. Your downshift control is safer than braking; though some of both may be wise if you are very careful in the use of your brakes, and avoid the hand brake. Shift your body weight to the rear this time; you should find this an instinctive move. If you must stop in a downhill position, plant your feet forward and solid, hold back on the handlebars and again grip the hand brake firmly. A gravity start before shifting into gear may appeal to you; but you risk jerking yourself forward as the gear engages, disrupting proper weight distribution. So again, get out of neutral into gear before starting forward, and take off slowly.

Because you need maximum traction on either an upgrade or downgrade, surface conditions are especially important. If you see sand blowing from a dump truck ahead as you begin to climb a hill, you at least are forewarned. If rain has made the hillside slick, you know the added danger. But if you start up a perfectly dry hill and assume the far side will be the same, you could be sorry. A recent oil spill could make it treacherous. Take all hills, up or down, as cautiously as you know how; and until you *know* what is on the other side, expect anything and be ready to protect yourself.

26. Reckless Motorist Hazards

I WOULD have to do no more than leave my home driveway to encounter a reckless motorist, depending on the timing—and there is no way of predicting when and where to expect a reckless driver to appear. Mine is a quiet residential neighborhood, according to real estate agents. Yet we get motorists during the day or night, at times, who will flash by at speeds up to 75 miles per hour. This is reckless driving by any standards; 30 miles per hour is the maximum authorized speed for this location.

Speeders

Speeders constitute one of the worst categories of reckless motorists; and they are to be found risking other people's lives along with their own at any hour and at any place where reason and emotional stability and alertness leave them while they are behind the wheel. Speeders come in all sizes, ages and physical conditions; drunk and sober; male and female; sane and otherwise; and they can be found in many different kinds of vehicles. The one thing they have in common is the fact that they come on the traffic scene with startling suddenness, and can wipe out a motorcycle rider easier than anyone except perhaps a pedestrian.

Your greatest protection is *not* your ability to jam into low and put on your own evasive burst of speed, although this is a positive protective move. Your greatest protection consists of your *alertness* (primarily involving your eyes and ears) and your *defensiveness*—riding constantly with the knowledge that speeders are a fact of life that must be *anticipated*. When you spot a vehicle in your rear-views overtaking you with unusual speed—or if an engine's roar from *any* direction tells you of a speeder's approach, *get out of the way!* Don't worry about appearing to be "chicken"; your job is to *stay alive*.

Stop-sign runners

In previous chapters, you have read case histories involving speeders and motorcycles; and the cyclists always came out the losers. Many more cases like them could be related; but the reckless driver violating other laws may pose an even greater threat to you. It was a motorist running a stop sign who caused a 26-year-old 350 cc operator to lose his life. The cyclist was wearing a helmet, but suffered three separate impacts as a result of this failure to yield. He was struck by the violator's car, a second car legally in motion, and then hit a stop sign at the corner.

A cycling couple aged 34 and 29 were going only 15–20 miles per hour on a 400 cc when they were struck by a car running a stop sign at 45–50 miles per hour. Three young people in the car were thrown out and injured. Both cyclists were killed after being ejected from the cycle for distances of 55 and 69 feet.

Misguided missile

A 37-year-old cycle rider collided with an oncoming car that had been approaching astraddle the centerline. Its driver suddenly turned in front of the cyclist and *stopped!* This motorist was drinking, and failed to yield to the oncoming cycle. He was charged with first degree manslaughter—real trouble. The biker was dead.

Expect the worst

In each of these three cases, the motorist was at fault by violating the traffic laws. In each case, cyclists died who might have escaped the accident by proper alertness and defensive riding. It has been stressed before, but can't be stressed too often: motorists *are* at fault more often than cyclists when these two vehicles collide. And knowing this, it's just good common sense on your part to ride fully alert to this possibility, and move accordingly. As I proceed down the street, I look at *every* oncoming car as one that might suddenly turn in front of me. The possible reason for such a move doesn't matter in the least; it's the *fact* of that possibility I keep in mind. *Expecting* the worst keeps me from being as *vulnerable* to it.

In the same way, I arrive at every intersection knowing that some motorist can fail to yield to me—for a variety of reasons that don't matter. My defense is in the knowing. When it happens, I'm ready for it, and can avoid the accident that would otherwise take place. When it doesn't happen, I don't kick myself inwardly for being an overly cautious fuddy-duddy; that would lead me to become careless and vulnerable the next time.

Drinkers—always reckless

In the last case cited, the motorist was driving under the influence of alcohol. It is a fact of life-and-death that motorists *do* drink and drive. And it is absolutely no protection that this is illegal. Your protection, again, is in your alertness and defensiveness. If you are in the vicinity of a beer joint, sharpen up; your chances of running into a drunk are increased. Ditto if you are riding after dark near night clubs. If you observe a motorist getting careless with the centerline or driving with a weaving rhythm, watch out for him; he could be drinking, sleepy or both. In any event he is a reckless driver—beware of him.

Compacts in the city

Much as I hate "putting labels on people," and generalizing, which always does an injustice to many, I will share my experience concerning two types of vehicles—each in a different locale. In the city, I have found from personal experience (both as a motorist and a cyclist) that the driver of the small "compact" auto is reckless more often than the law of averages should allow. I have no statistics to support this observation; but I have learned to use extra caution around compacts.

Pickups in the country

In the rural areas, as might be expected, the pickup truck is most often involved in accidents. It's logical because the pickup is the most common vehicle on rural roads. I have also had pickup owners complain about more blind-spot trouble than they find in other vehicles. Pickup drivers tend to drive faster than the law allows; and failure to yield when leaving a section-line road to enter a highway seems almost to be a "way of life" in low-traffic rural areas. Rural drivers you meet are more apt to be under legal licensing age; and this means less maturity in driving judgment, and perhaps in ability.

On a motorcycle, you simply have to ride more alert and more defensively in rural areas. You'll encounter "slow-moving" vehicles there (tractors and other farm implement vehicles); ride cautiously near them. They should be marked with a fire-orange triangle at the rear for good visibility; but don't depend on it.

Just plain mean

I reported the following incident more briefly in an earlier chapter; but it deserves inclusion in any discussion of reckless motorists. If I hadn't witnessed it myself, I wouldn't have believed it. Southbound on a four-lane expressway after working hours one day, I was clocking about 55 not far behind another cyclist. Traffic was heavy, but seemed to be moving well until I saw a car moving up fast in my left rear-view mirror. I watched as it sped past, suddenly darted in between me and the cycle ahead, then proceeded to deliberately crowd the guy all the way off onto the shoulder (he continued down an exit ramp).

Why the driver of the car, whose three passengers seemed to enjoy the whole thing, picked on the cyclist ahead instead of me, I don't know. I've wondered if they knew the guy and were either out to get even for something or "have fun" with him (some fun!). I really hate to think there are people in the world who would pick on just any cyclist they take a fancy to, and run him off the road. Regardless, this is one more category of reckless motorist to beware: the one who is deliberately antagonistic towards motorcycle riders. Your protective measures are the same as those for approaching speeders. Be *alert*; ride *defensively*; and if you even suspect they can be a personal hazard, *get out of their way!*

Who, me signal?

One indication that a driver may tend to be reckless and should be carefully watched, is when he fails to give the required signals. If a person thinks it's "square" to signal when he plans to turn, change driving lanes or stop, chances are better than 50–50 he will also drive recklessly in other ways. The same holds true for the motorist you see passing on curves, hills or in other no-passing zones. *Avoid* him; he's reckless and dangerous.

27. Highway Hazards

T<small>HE</small> American Driver and Traffic Safety Education Association (a department of the National Education Association) says:

"The rider is most vulnerable to injury in highway traffic. If the novice rider is to operate safely in a complex highway environment congested with vehicles of larger sizes and various performance ranges, he must be trained in a program which stresses behaviors required for operating a motorcycle on public highways. For the motorcyclist to ride safely, he must, at a minimum, (1) recognize problems associated with vehicle mix in the highway transportation system, (2) be familiar with basic types of motorcycles and riding environments, (3) be especially aware of the potential hazards to the motorcyclist, and (4) be familiar with strategies to cope with those hazards."

In my state, nearly two-thirds of all fatal motor vehicle accidents during a recent year took place on county, state or federal highways. I can't really recommend the highways as being safe for joyriding by cyclists. I know families of four who take to the highways annually on long cross-country trips on big cycles and love it; they say they have never had an accident on these jaunts. I also know of a local couple, long-time riders of smaller bikes, who finally saved enough to buy big road bikes for each of them and took off for a long-awaited touring vacation. On the first day out the husband helplessly witnessed his wife's death on the highway in an accident caused by a motorist.

Most of my own experience has been off the highway, for the simple reason that I bought and use my cycle for in-town "commuter" purposes: job transportation, errands—all of the going which doesn't involve passengers or bulky packages.

Bike size does count

I have taken to the highways on occasion; and my wife, being a good sport, has grabbed a helmet and gone with me as much as 160 miles round trip. But she would prefer not doing it again. My 200 cc street bike just wasn't made for that kind of travel; and neither of us was made for that kind of mechanical vibes and wind blasts (I have no fairings). Even if I move up to a 400 cc twin next time (likely, now that both the 200 cc and 350 cc have been discontinued by the factory), it will still be a little light for highway comfort and safety.

Here are a few tips from those who have mixed it up on the state and interstate highways, and who might think nothing of vacationing on two wheels for a couple of thousand miles.

Get to know the heavies

First off, as I have indicated, it's no place for the lightweight around-towners, regardless of the pretty color pictures in the sales brochures. The machine wasn't made for it; and before you realize it, the vibration can almost render your forearms numb—and other parts of your anatomy as well. When you select a larger bike for whatever purpose, whether you borrow, rent or buy it, it will be unfamiliar to you. It makes no difference if you are an experienced rider on a lighter cycle of the same make; practice like a rank beginner until you get the hang of it. Then and only then will you be at all safe in putting it in a highway traffic stream.

If I wanted to take to the highways on a 750 cc or larger, I would take at least a day or two of practice riding before making the highway trip. I would talk to highway riders about the machine differences, and things to watch out for on a long, high-speed run that I don't run into at slower speeds on city streets. I would check with my dealer and try getting the name of someone who has made cycle trips to the *area* I plan to visit, to get some routing and wind condition tips.

Truck wind hazards

There are special hazards on the highway that only extra caution and experience will help you to meet successfully. An approaching truck traveling at a high rate of speed can literally sweep you off your machine by the wind velocity in creates. If you overtake a big truck/trailer rig, the vortex of wind and vacuum developed at its rear can drag you down in an uncontrollable and disastrous spill.

Have your bike in shape

Be *certain* your machine is in top condition, including excellent tires. You will want to stiffen the steering if your cycle has a damper. This will give you optimum steering control; but be sure to back off the setting when you arrive at your destination and resume slower speeds. This adjustment/readjustment procedure will make for safer riding. It avoids high speed wobble, and the tendency towards sway that can happen at slower speeds with stiff steering.

Higher speeds hazard

Highway traffic moves at higher speeds than most street cyclists are accustomed to; motorists often exceed the 55-miles-per-hour speed limit as though it didn't exist. Keep in mind that at 60 miles per hour, it will take these drivers from 265 to 325 feet to react to an emergency and come to a stop, depending on their individual ability and the condition of their brakes. This fact and the frequency of rear-end collisions underline the importance of using your three-second (slow two-count) system to give you the necessary safe-distance separation from other vehicles as you travel the highways.

Keep your distance

One legally licensed 14-year-old was tailgating a well-service truck on a U.S. highway while riding a 125 cc. Unaware of an oncoming pickup being driven at excessive speed, the boy made a sharp left turn to exit onto a county road. The pickup laid down 52 feet of skid marks before the impact, and 171 feet afterwards. The cyclist, carried 173 feet from the point of collision, died at the scene.

Rural hazards

Highway travel means travel in rural areas, and this brings a new set of hazards into play: more risk from loose animals that can appear suddenly on the roadway, or run into a vehicle from the side of the highway; more drivers who are less alert because they are accustomed to meeting fewer vehicles; more drivers who have diminished reflexes due to going long stretches without proper rest; more chance of encountering underage, inexperienced drivers. (Many farm children are given driving privileges by their parents before actually reaching the legal age. This goes for motorcycling permission as well as being allowed to drive a pickup truck or other motorized equipment.)

A case history in support of my last point was a fatal accident involving three children whose ages *totaled* 29 years. An 8-year-old boy was operating a 75 cc trail bike on the highway, with his 6-year-old sister riding as a passenger. A pickup driven at a speed of 55 miles per hour by an unlicensed 15-year-old struck the cyclists, skidding 30 feet before and 70 feet after the impact. The cycle operator was killed and his sister was badly injured. The children, of course, should not have been operating the vehicles, and should not have been on the highway. The cycle was not legal for the highway, and not legal for passengers. If you had been overtaken by the 15-year-old, even if you were licensed and were riding a highway-worthy machine, you might have had trouble avoiding being overrun. Highway travel requires special alertness because of special hazards.

Plan your trip well

Your highway trip will be safer if you plan it well. Dress properly for any weather contingency. Take the tools, spare parts and other equipment you may need for emergencies. Because there are so many CB radio operators on the highways today, a simple felt-tip pen and a rolled sheet of white paper might get help for you when needed. Just use the pen to draw a large, attention-getting "10-34" on the paper, and hold it up to passing motorists. Any experienced CB'er will know you have run into trouble and need assistance, upon reading that coded message. A road flare takes up little space, and can be invaluable.

Plan your specific route carefully, including frequent rest stops, refueling points, and early stops for the day where you can rest comfortably. If you are riding with other cyclists, agree on a reasonable speed and separation distance, and maintain them. Don't ride two abreast, even if there is one lane per cycle. Stagger your positions, in pairs, with the lead cycle and other odd-numbered bikers riding in the left-third position. Leave passing room (pull-in space) between each pair. Pass other vehicles only as recommended in Chapter 20. Keep a constant check on the cycle behind you, as well as the traffic ahead. Arrange suitable signals before you start, for necessary communications as you travel.

It's always a good idea to give yourself extra visibility in highway traffic, with fluorescent jackets or striping securely attached to saddlebags or other practical surfaces.

Steady does it

Avoid unnecessary lane changing, and maintain a steady pace. If you find yourself alongside another vehicle traveling in another lane at your speed, don't continue to block the highway; change your lane, your speed, or both to break the bottleneck.

Hypnosis hazard

As you ride the highway, don't suffer the hypnosis hazard—a greater danger here than in city riding. Keep your eyes on the move, not fixed on any one object more than a second or two at a time. Don't forget to keep a watchful eye on entry and exit points intersecting the highway. A 39-year-old riding a 350 cc cycle was struck by a truck as it pulled off of a county dirt road onto the state highway in front of the cyclist. The setting sun may have been in the trucker's eyes, according to the fatality report. As the person in greatest jeopardy, it will be *your* responsibility to know when someone is entering your highway—and know they see you and are yielding to you—before you pass the entry point.

Stay right and ready

If you are on a multiple-lane highway, keep to the right except for passing, and do that with extreme care. Don't relax your rear-view mirror habit, either. You'll need them for passing, knowing when you're about to be passed, and when pulling off the highway. *Any* time you find yourself in a braking position, check the rear-views at the first possible moment. You could be in danger from a less-than-alert overtaking motorist. Be ready to take evasive action, even if only by taking up a little of the slack you've put between yourself and the vehicle ahead. This will give the driver behind you more stopping time; but if it appears to be necessary, don't hesitate to take to the shoulder.

Stay off the median; if you need to turn back, go on to the next official crossing point and do it safely.

Ride by day

Night riding may be cool and pleasant; but neither you nor the motorists around you can see well enough to insure that it will be safe. Here's a case history stressing this point—involving three boys aged 15 and under. Two of them were riding after dark without any lights, and with no license, no cycle tag and no helmets. They pulled left of the centerline of a county highway, directly into a head-on collision with a brother of the operator. This brother was also riding a cycle—in the opposite direction. All three cyclists were injured, and one of the brothers died.

28. If Your Cycle Stops Running

D ON'T underestimate the importance of the advice contained in this, the shortest chapter of the book. The three case histories given here are all too typical of needless fatalities that occur every year when a rider's cycle stops running and the proper measures aren't taken.

We'll take a look at possible reasons why your motorcycle might quit on you, and what you can do to get underway again. But first and foremost, here's the big thing to remember to save your life:

> If your cycle stops running, *get it off the roadway immediately!*
> Do this without exception, even if you know what the problem
> is, and think you can correct it while rolling.

Bear in mind, I'm not telling you to pull off and start over again if your machine is simply *threatening* to quit because fuel is running out in the main tank. You need to have the ability to reach down without taking your eyes off the traffic, switch your fuel tank to reserve and go right ahead as the engine recovers its liquid nutrition. But if the engine has actually quit, get out of the way *now!* I'll underscore this advice with three recent cyclist fatalities from highway patrol records.

The first case began when two men, aged 24 and 34, borrowed a big cycle for a highway run. It stopped on a hill, just short of the crest. A car being driven about 50–55 miles per hour came over the hill from the opposite direction. Only two things caused the accident: the oncoming car topped the hill on the wrong side of the centerline; and the two cyclists were still in the roadway, trying to restart their machine. Both cyclists were killed in the crash in which both the car and the cycle burned.

You *can* say that if the automobile driver had stayed on his side of the highway, the cyclists would not have died. What I insist on saying is that people *do* drive like that at times, and if you want to stay alive, you won't risk the odds by hoping your breakdown will not be one of those times. If your cycle stops running, get it off the roadway *immediately!*

In the next case, a 25-year-old rider was pushing his bike to a service station after running out of gas. If you, like him, are right-handed, you know just how he was doing it: walking on the left side of the cycle, near the right edge of the street. A speeding car (50 miles per hour in a 35-miles-per-hour zone) struck him and knocked him 68 feet to his death.

You *can* say that if the motorist had not been speeding, the cyclist would not have died. Again I say, people *do* drive like that at times; and this was one of the times.

Last case. A 16-year-old with his life ahead of him, pushing a 185 cc that had quit on him as he rode along a state highway at night. Dead cycle, no lights—an obviously hazardous situation, right? But not obvious enough for this rider to get off the highway, onto the four-foot shoulder the state had provided for emergencies. When his death car came along, it hurled his body 191 feet.

You *might* say that with the proper rear reflectors and a fluorescent jacket and helmet, the motorcycle rider could have been seen by the motorist in spite of the unlit cycle. What I say again is important to your survival. If your cycle stops running, get it off the roadway *immediately!*

Diagnosis and cure

Why would your cycle stop running in the first place? If you take the advice of Chapter 3, chances are it wouldn't. A fit machine is the only kind to ride anytime, and particularly on a highway trip. If you plan your trip properly, you'll stop in plenty of time to refuel; so you shouldn't run out of gas. But you may have a bike that cuts out abruptly when your main tank goes dry. If that's the case, *get off the roadway,* and switch to the reserve tank. Restart and be on your way.

You might accidentally hit your kill switch, or knock your fuel valve to the OFF position. If that's the case, *get off the roadway,* reposition the button or valve and restart.

You might have too little oil, fouled spark plugs, a clogged fuel tank cap air vent or an overheated engine. If so, *get off the roadway* and scrape your plugs or let your engine cool; then restart and go on.

In the latter cases, you can readily see why you need to get off the roadway to correct the problem. But you may be asking "Why?" if it's merely a case of switching to the reserve tank or repositioning the kill switch. If your engine has actually quit, there will have to be a reignition following your valve switching or button repositioning move. You may or may *not* handle this smoothly, with the proper clutching action, in the stress of the moment. The *safe* thing to do is to first get out of the way of those impatient motorists and shift into neutral. Next, correct your problem, restart and take off calmly when the way is perfectly clear.

Downhill or push starting

It is possible to restart your cycle on a downgrade or with a push, if your problem is a weak battery. Get in the saddle, turn your ignition key on; put your bike into second or third gear (for a less forceful start); squeeze your clutch lever. When the downgrade run or the push *by a second party* generates sufficient momentum, ease out the clutch lever for the engine start. You may or may not wish to pull out your choke lever for this operation, depending on whether vapor-lock may have been your problem. If you use a downhill run for your start, wait until all traffic clears. Same thing when someone is pushing you; and thank them in advance, not by turning around in your saddle and waving after the startup.

In case your cycle simply won't restart, remember that "10-34" sign for flagging down help from CB'ers—it works.

Now—what's the *first* thing to do if your cycle stops running? Good! You got the message.

29. Expect the Unexpected

EVERYTHING this book tries to teach is aimed at the life-saving goal of riding defensively—*super* defensively, if you will. One of the most valuable courses you can take is a "Defensive Driving" course, such as you will find sponsored by your State Highway Patrol. It helps tremendously for anyone who wants to stay alive on a street cycle to learn defensive automobile driving measures, and vice versa. The safer and more defensively you operate a motorcycle, the better you will be as a defensive motorist behind the wheel of a car.

Defensive driving course

In a defensive driving course, you will learn to drive more flexibly, willing to give up your right-of-way to avoid an accident; be able to cope with the illogical and unexpected actions of other drivers and pedestrians; drive with an awareness of your vehicle's mechanical limitations; and know how to tailor your driving to the constantly changing road and traffic conditions, weather, etc. In such a course, you will be taught to *expect* the "unexpected" any time you ride into traffic.

Check with your Highway Patrol or the nearest office of the National Safety Council to get details of defensive driving courses available in your area. Almost everything you learn in this motorist-oriented course will serve you well as a motorcycle operator.

When you arrive at the point of knowing that what "can't happen" can kill you, and operate your bike accordingly, you're on your way to surviving in traffic on a motorcycle. You must realize that "the other guy" is entirely capable at any time of pulling a stunt that is either idiotic, illegal or impossible.

In researching for this book, I walked into the records division of the State Department of Public Safety. When an attractive young lady asked if she could help me, I gave her my name and told her what I was working on. Casting her eyes ceilingward, she turned to the lady at the next desk, who said to me *"Tell* us about it!" Her husband, a long-time cyclist, had just been rear-ended by an inebriated motorist who followed his cycle right off the street onto the shoulder and ran him down in a "where you go, I go" maneuver that couldn't have been predicted.

Similar actions are, however, on record. One of the fatal accidents in the files of that office from recent years involved the *deliberate* rear-ending of a 17-year-old 350 cc rider. A pickup driver "under the influence" ran over the boy (who was riding at 45 miles per hour) while speeding at 80 miles per hour. The cyclist was knocked over 176 feet and killed by this senseless act.

What *can* be done, then, about senseless acts that can't be predicted? I suggest you thoroughly drill yourself to *expect* the *unexpected*. For these rear-ending hazards, reread Chapter 23. The only advice I have is there and in the title of *this* chapter.

On that same day of my first research visit to the Highway Patrol, the trooper who gives motorcycle safety training to the public showed me some photographs of a fatality scene. In this case, a cyclist topped a rise at a pretty good clip only to be confronted by a brush pile right out on the little-traveled street. He had no time to avoid the hazard, which flipped the rider and sent the bike out of control. It hurtled across the street and crashed into a *parked* Highway Patrol cruiser whose trooper had just then spotted the brush and was radioing for its removal.

That poor rider couldn't be expected to know about the hazard; but he *could* have crested that rise at a safe, controllable speed if he had learned to *expect* the *unexpected*.

Ride your cycle with the sure knowledge that there are times when anything that *can* go wrong *will*. You can't mount a crystal ball on your handlebars; you can't read the minds of motorists in the traffic around you. But you can operate your bike as alertly as a soldier in a booby-trapped, sniper-infested jungle—*not* like a joyrider without a care in the world. When you ride on the streets and highways, it *is* a jungle and the snipers *are* near. If this sounds so grim you want to forget you ever saw a motorcycle, I'm sorry; that's not my goal. The trick is to achieve a constant alertness *without* losing your ability to enjoy the whole thing; if I can do it, *you* can do it.

Expecting the unexpected is the same thing as anticipating the *possible*. Like the sudden rush of a vehicle-chasing dog, from behind a hedge; or a child coming "out of nowhere" just as quickly. This happened to a 23-year-old 250 cc bike rider. An 8-year-old boy wheeled out of a side street on a bicycle and glided right across the centerline into the path of the motorcycle. In this case it was the boy who was killed; the heavier vehicle the victor as usual. But the older cycle rider must have died a little inside; and the intersection alertness called for in previous chapters was the preventive precaution this situation demanded.

Even those car doors being opened in your face might be unexpected; but they *shouldn't be.* This is the kind of hazard you must learn to anticipate, and be alert for.

You probably won't be expecting your throttle to stick, or your clutch cable to break. But both of these things do happen. Reread Chapters 3 and 17, and know what to do *if* it happens to you. Meanwhile, ride as though you believe it *will* happen to you, and you'll be riding more safely.

That brush pile in the street probably bounced off the back of some truck hauling it to the dump, without the driver's knowledge. There are *many* insecure loads that can drop into your path while you are following a truck. Just be sure you're not following *too closely* when it happens, and that you are actually *expecting* something to fall off.

Wrong-way drivers

Here's an unexpected hazard for you. Normally you have a right to expect that all traffic in the westbound lanes of a street or highway will be westbound. The problem is, some people drive in an *abnormal* manner at times. You have already read about two young cyclists who died in a head-on crash while trying to elude a pursuing police officer. They had deliberately crossed an expressway median and were proceeding westbound against eastbound traffic. In Wyoming on that same day, a 60-year-old man heading east in an interstate highway westbound lane smashed his car head-on into a car properly heading west in the same lane. He was killed; so were three women in the other vehicle.

These may have been the only two wrong-way accidents in the nation on that particular day; but I doubt it. According to the National Safety Council, the U.S. has about 100,000 "left-of-centerline" accidents every year. How many of these are wrong-way accidents is not revealed in their report; but here in Oklahoma during a recent single year, there were 140 *wrong-way* collisions. If we were average for the 50 states, there would be about 7,000 annually; about 19 per day. Too many to be classified as extreme rarities, certainly. It not only *can* happen here, it *does* happen. One more good reason to ride your two-wheeler alert to *anything*—*expecting* the unexpected.

Tire blowouts

Tire blowouts must be included in the list of unexpected hazards; but I hope you don't *expect* one of these. If you do, you're ignoring personal safety. Expecting a blowout just means you are guilty of criminal negligence with the only thing between you and the surface you're riding upon: your tires. I have heard of a blowout on a brand new cycle; but I don't have it confirmed. I've never had any tire problems of any kind and pray I never do. Speaking of prayer, that would be the best thing I can recommend if you *do* have a blowout. Depending on your speed, surface and traffic situation, it could easily end your cycling career.

If you have a blowout that isn't too severe, you can come through it with the least possible damage if you *don't apply your brakes.* Just let off the throttle and slow down gradually, moving off the roadway as soon as it can be done carefully, at *low speed.* Keep a firm grip on your handlebars while all this is going on, to give you a little better control.

Well, good friends and fellow cyclists, that's about all the tips and advice I can give you out of my own experience, and from the "brain-picking" job I've done with others who have ridden much longer than I. I'm convinced it all boils down to two things: how *smart* you are, and how much you *want to stay alive.* If you're smart enough to take good advice, smart enough to really learn and *put into practice* the safety information in this book, you *can* stay alive in traffic on a motorcycle, and enjoy your two-wheeling experience for just about as many years as you like. But besides being smart, you have to possess the *will to live.* You must want to live enough to ride safely while you see your peers ride like lunatics. Or you can join them with the odds in favor of your joining them in the cemetery sooner or later.

Time after time in these pages, you have read actual case histories taken from the Oklahoma Highway Patrol records. You can find more of the same in your own state's records. Case histories of fatalities caused by *willful* speeding; riding while under the influence of alcohol; overriding cycle lights at night; and taking other ridiculous risks that simply don't make sense for anyone interested in staying alive.

Wanting to live is entirely up to *you*; and if your reaction to what you have just read is negative, you have flunked the exams on both the will to live and intelligence. Hang up your helmet, if you have one, and get yourself four wheels tied together with 4,000 pounds of steel!

Special cycling license

I firmly hope and believe the day will come when anyone who wants to ride a motorcycle on the streets and highways will be required to obtain a special license. That license, specifically for cycle operation, will be issued only after qualified training successfully completed, and evidence of physical fitness and good mental attitude. The motorcycle, too, will be subject to regular annual safety inspection, regardless of state.

I *hope* that as the number of registered motorcycles continues to grow in this country at the rate of a half million per year, motorists will become increasingly alert and amenable to them in traffic. The current surge of interest in mopeds, whose riders will have all of the hazards of street traffic without the power capability for evasive action, also makes this imperative. (See the next chapter for more on mopeds.) It may be that traffic citations issued in cycle-auto accidents will have to be made twice as costly before some of the problems of motorist culpability begin to lessen appreciably.

30. The Pros and Cons About Mopeds

A QUICK look is all I care to take, where mopeds are concerned. Admittedly, they have caught my eye from the money viewpoint; they're both cheap to buy and more inexpensive to operate than any two-wheeler except a bicycle. With top mileage-economy automobiles boasting about 40 miles per gallon on the highway, mopeds will take you 125–150 miles in the city on that same gallon.

But having said that, and added that mopeds are "fun" to ride as long as you manage to stay out of trouble, I find little else that can be said for them. I'm well aware that moped manufacturers and dealers claim they are "safer than motorcycles." I suppose from the standpoint that you'll never find anyone exceeding the speed limit on a moped, there might be some truth to the claim. But by the same token, moped operators can't generate enough speed to take evasive action in an emergency brought about by the driver of some *other* vehicle using the same roadway. As for motorcycle accidents, greater safety is achievable simply through the proper mind-set and safety-oriented actions of the rider. The underpowered moped is in my judgment something of a road hazard in itself; I won't trust my life to one.

What is a moped?

It's something more than a bicycle and less than a motorcycle. It is a two-wheeler equipped with a motor of no more than 50 cc. You can pedal it like a bicycle (though not as easily or as far); in fact, you *do* pedal it to get started. Then you switch on its small engine (2 hp max) and let it carry you at speeds up to 30 miles per hour on level streets. On a steep hill, your moped will slow to a point where you'll have to add leg-power to reach the top, or stall out altogether and force you to take to the side of the road and walk it to another start-ing place. Moped speeds vary with the weight of the rider, but as a rule are so slow that motorists impatiently whip around the "wee beastie" in traffic. If you can't keep pace and a motorist on your tail can't pass, he just might crowd you to the curb.

If you give serious thought to buying a moped, take a good test drive first. Too many of the seats will be uncomfortable for you, forcing you into a tiring posture. You may also find the ride stiff and jolting. Check the brakes independently and as a team; and note the practicality (or *lack* of it) of the horn and rear-view mirror. If the mirror vibrates enough to blur your vision, and the horn gives out the bleat of a newborn lamb, both will have to be replaced for safety.

Traction on mopeds is too easily lost. Some makes are unstable on turns; and in turning on a gravel-coated surface, "traction became marginal at about 15 miles per hour" on 10 models tested.

Are the lights big enough to attract attention? Does the moped come equipped with turn signals? Too often the answer will be no to both these questions. Signaling by hand gets to be a little tricky in view of the fact that the front brake is activated by your right hand. And by the way, mopeds usually come without batteries; such horn and lights as you have will operate only while the engine is running, and their output will vary with your speed. Again, not the safest con-dition you could have.

What are the laws governing mopeds?

As of this writing, state laws vary widely, with a handful still classify-ing them as motorcycles and requiring moped owners to be licensed, insured and meet operating regulations accordingly. Most states re-quire either an automobile driver's license or a special license. Most do *not* require liability insurance or the wearing of a helmet; but most states require mopeds to be registered.

Some facts about moped safety

Most of the statistics concerning moped accidents come to us from European countries where the critter was born, and often makes up a third of all vehicular traffic. Across the national boundaries, methods of reporting vary; so the statistics available are valuable primarily to project a broad picture, and indicate the hazard potential for moped operators in the United States. One should keep in mind that the use of mopeds in Europe is primarily as a means of getting to and from school and work, as opposed to the pleasure/recreational use which is dominant in this country.

The findings that follow here are excerpted from an analysis of mopeds as a potential safety problem, published by the U.S. Department of Transportation in May 1979.

Citing a study by the European Conference of Ministers of Transport, the report states, "although accounting for only 17 percent of the two-wheeled vehicles represented in the participating nations, mopeds accounted for 50 percent of the injuries and 43 percent of the fatalities in accidents involving either mopeds, bicycles or motorcycles."

A look at accident data from France, Switzerland and the Netherlands is especially pertinent, since the moped is used in such great numbers there, compared to other vehicles. One ECMT study of total road deaths revealed the following percentages accounted for by two-wheeled vehicles:

	BICYCLES	MOPEDS	MOTORCYCLES
France	4.6	16.6	3.3
Switzerland	7.0	11.0	9.8
Netherlands	17.3	19.0	3.0

The same study showed mopeds accounting for 74.7% of all 2WV (two-wheel vehicles) injuries, and 67.8% of all 2WV deaths in France; 45.4% and 39.6% respectively in Switzerland; and 70.4% and 48.3% respectively in the Netherlands.

Three years after the ECMT study, another made by H. Loeffelholz and F. Nicklisch for the Federal Highway Institute in Germany showed similar results for these countries of concentrated moped usage. Again, the figures that follow represent the percentage of total road casualties (both deaths and injuries in this case) accounted for by the various 2WV's:

	BICYCLES	MOPEDS	MOTORCYCLES
France	3	15	3
Switzerland	7	14	11
Netherlands	15	35	3

Note that well over a third of Netherlands traffic deaths and injuries involve the moped. Casualties there have been increasing steadily since 1960, keeping pace with the increased mileage exposure.

The bad news about moped statistics is not confined to the highest-usage European countries. In Sweden, where mopeds account for only three percent of the estimated total road mileage, they account for *seven* percent of the fatal accidents. London metropolitan police found that for most of the 1970's, moped casualties consistently accounted for 15 to 20 percent of the city's serious-injury or fatal road accidents. In Finland, the moped is involved in 4.5 times as many fatal accidents as passenger cars; 1.4 times as many as motorcycles. In another study from West Germany, using actual mileage as the denominator term, the moped group appears to be 10–12 times more accident-prone than the automobile group. In Belgium since 1973, bicycle fatalities have decreased about ten percent. During the same period, motorcycle fatalities have increased about eight percent. But moped fatalities are up 15%!

I fear the European experience with mopeds is a valid harbinger of what will take place in the United States as more and more are purchased and taken onto our streets. Mopeds are being touted here as somewhat ideal for our senior citizens who need economical transportation for shopping and other short trips. But in Europe, older riders consistently account for an unduly large number of accidents on mopeds.

Yes, the moped is cheap to buy, simple to operate and fantastically economical. But if you're interested in *safety* on two wheels, I'm personally not convinced that a moped is the way to go. Neither is one California highway patrolman who says, "In almost all collisions, the operator of a moped ends up in a hospital." Well, you say, the same thing is true of motorcycle operators. I won't argue that point; I simply say that when I ride a two-wheeler, I want enough power to take evasive action in emergencies when I can. If you *do* buy a moped, follow the safety tips in this book.

No matter what kind of cycle you operate on streets and highways, the major burden for your safety will rest squarely on your own shoulders. I hope I have made it clear that staying alive on a motorcycle is primarily a matter under your control. You now know the risks, and how to avoid them. Putting this knowledge into practice is up to you. SAFE RIDING!

APPENDICES

REFERENCE SOURCES

1. National Safety Council. "Motorcycle Facts" (*Sept. 1978*)
2. Motorcycle Safety Foundation. "Motorcycle Statistics" (*1978*)
3. "Motorcycle Accident Research"—Study sponsored by the Motorcycle Safety Foundation and presented by Martin L. Reiss, BioTechnology, Inc. at the Foundation's Motorcycle Operator Testing Workshop (*Oct. 1974*)
4. Kraus, Riggins, Drysdale and Franti report to 100th Annual Meeting of the American Public Health Association, Atlantic City, New Jersey (*Nov. 1974*)
5. Oklahoma Department of Public Safety. "Motorcycle Accident Facts" (*1978*)
6. National Safety Council. "Safety Education Data Sheet No. 98, Revised"
7. American Driver and Traffic Safety Education Association. "Motorcycle Safety Education: On-street Riders" (*1974*)
8. Motorcycle Safety Foundation. "Analysis of Motorcycle Accident Statistics" (*Mar. 1978*)
9. Consumer Reports (*June 1978*)
10. U.S. Department of Transportation. "The Effect of Motorcycle Helmet Usage on Head Injuries" (*Jan. 1979*)
11. U.S. Department of Transportation. "Motorcycle Helmets: Claims & Facts" (*Jan. 1978*)
12. National Highway Traffic Safety Administration. "Motorcycle Accident Cause Factors" (*Jan. 1979*)
13. National Highway Traffic Safety Administration. "Motorcycle Accident Data Summary" (*1979*)

GLOSSARY OF TERMS

Black side, the tires of a motorcycle

cc, cubic centimeters; a measurement of combustion-chamber volume of motorcycles or mopeds, and indicative of the power/speed capabilities

Chopper, modified motorcycle featuring an extended, slanted front fork

Commuter, one of the lower-powered "street" motorcycles designed for work/school/errands transportation; the rider of such a cycle

Damper, device by which motorcycle operator can alter the steering/shock-absorbing action for either city or highway travel

Fairing, plastic windshield for motorcycle use

Fishtailing, side-to-side motion of motorcycle rear wheel, caused by uncoordinated stop, rough or slick surface, or both

Grab bar, passenger hand-hold attached at the rear of motorcycle saddle

Horses, horsepower rating of motorcycle engine

Kill switch, instant engine shutoff switch, usually red and mounted atop a handlebar near one grip

Leathers, pants and/or jacket of leather providing maximum motorcycle rider protection in the event of a spill

Lifting a left, motorcycle riders' greeting when approaching each other while riding

Minibike, motorcycle of extremely small size, very limited power, and generally not equipped or licensable for anything but single-passenger, off-street use

Moped, hybrid-characteristics two-wheeler that must be pedaled to generate start-up momentum for the attached mini-motor of 50cc or less; limited by law to a maximum 30 miles per hour

Pegs, motorcycle foot rests

Peripheral vision, ability to detect movements and objects to the right or left, with eyes straight ahead

Rev, accelerate speed

Shiny side, top side of a motorcycle

Skid-lid, crash helmet

Slant-fork, "chopper" (see definition)

Street cycle/street-legal, motorcycle of sufficient size, power, and with proper equipment for authorized use of streets and highways along with other motorized vehicular traffic

Stripes riding, maneuvering ahead in traffic by riding a motorcycle between legal lanes

Suicycle, any powered two-wheeler operated without regard to the safety tips incorporated in this book

Twin, 2-carburetor cycle

Two-wheeler, vehicle classification including motorcycles, mopeds, motorized scooters and bicycles

Wheelie, act of balancing a two-wheel vehicle on the rear wheel while moving forward

ASSOCIATIONS/ORGANIZATIONS/AGENCIES

American Driver and Traffic Safety Education Association
1201 Sixteenth St., N.W., Washington, DC 20036

American Motorcyclist Association
P.O. Box 141, Westerville, OH 43081

BioTechnology, Inc.
3027 Rosemary Lane, Falls Church, VA 22046

Insurance Institute for Highway Safety
Watergate 600, Washington, DC 20037

Moped Association of America
1001 Connecticut Ave., N.W., Rm. 707, Washington, DC 20036

Motorcycle Industry Council
4100 Birch St., Suite 101, Newport Beach, CA 92660

Motorcycle Safety Foundation
780 Elkridge Landing Road, Linthicum, MD 21090

National Motorcycle Dealers Association
100 Vermont Ave., N.W., Washington, DC 20005

National Safety Council
444 North Michigan Ave., Chicago, IL 60611

Traffic Engineering & Safety Dept., American Automobile Association
1712 G Street, N.W., Washington, DC 20006

U.S. Dept. of Transportation, National Highway Safety Administration
400 Seventh St., N.W., Washington, DC 20590

American Motorcyclist (AMA News)
American Motorcyclist Association, 33 Collegeview Rd., Westerville, OH 43081

Big Bike
Hi-Torque Publications, Inc., 16200 Ventura Blvd., Encino, CA 91316

Biker Newsmagazine
Cycle News, Inc., Box 2610, 2499 Cerritos Ave., Long Beach, CA 90806

Cycle (and Cycle Buyers Guide)
Ziff-Davis, One Park Ave., New York, New York 10016

Cycle Guide
Quinn Publications, Inc., 1440 W. Walnut, Compton, CA 90220

Cycle News East (and Cycle News West)
Cycle News, Inc., 2201 Cherry Ave., Long Beach, CA 90806

Cycle World
CBS Publications, 1499 Monrovia Ave., Newport Beach, CA 92663

Easyriders
Paisano Publications, Inc., 819 South Glenoaks Blvd., Burbank, CA 91502

Modern Cycle
Modern Cycle Publishing Co., Inc., 7805 Deering Ave., Canoga Park, CA 91304

Moped Biking
Moped Publications, Inc., 370 Lexington Ave., New York, NY 10017

Motorcycle World
Country Wide Publications, 257 Park Ave., S., New York, NY 10010

Motorcyclist
Petersen Publications Co., Inc., 8490 Sunset Blvd., Los Angeles, CA 90069

Popular Cycling
Coronado Book Co., 12301 Wilshire Blvd., Los Angeles, CA 90025

Rider
Trailer Life Publishing Co., Inc., 23945 Craftsman Rd., Calabasas, CA 91302

Road Rider
2201 Laguna Canyon Rd., Box 678 Laguna Beach, CA 92677

Touring Bike
4247 La Palma Ave., Anaheim, CA 92806

STATE MOTORCYCLE
EQUIPMENT REQUIREMENTS
JANUARY 1979

MOTORCYCLE INDUSTRY COUNCIL, INC.

This information is provided by the Motorcycle Industry Council Government Relations office. As State Assemblies continue to pass and/or amend motorcycle equipment requirements, subsequent charts with current dates will be issued. Phone, telex, or write to the

Motorcycle Industry Council offices listed below for additional information concerning motorcycle equipment requirements or for additional copies of this chart.

STATE	SAFETY HELMET	EYE PROTECTION	REARVIEW MIRROR	BRAKES	HANDLEBAR HEIGHT	PASSENGER SEAT	PASSENGER FOOTRESTS	PASSENGER HANDHOLD	SAFETY BARS	PROTECTIVE CLOTHING	TURN SIGNALS	SPEEDOMETER/ODOMETER	HEADLIGHT DAYTIME USE	PERIODIC INSPECTION
Alabama	●			●-7		●	●				●			
Alaska	●-22	●-i	●-6	●-8	●-13	●	●							
Arizona	●-3	●-h		●-7	●-13	●	●							●-19
Arkansas	●		●	●-7		●	●	●	●					
California	●		●	●-8	●-14	●	●	●			●		■-k	●-21
Colorado		●	●	●-7		●	●	●						●
Connecticut		●-h		●-8g	●-13	●	●	●						●-21
Delaware	■-1,m	●		●-7	●-13	●	●	●			●			●
Dist. of Col.	●	●-h		●-8	●-13	●	●	●				●-17		●
Florida	●	●		●-8	●-13	●	●						●	
Georgia	●	●-h	●-5	●-7		●	●			●-16			●	
Hawaii	●-1,3	●-h		●-7	●-13	●	●						●	
Idaho	■-3			●-7		●	●							
Illinois	●	●		●-7	●-13	●	●	●						
Indiana			●-5	●-8	●-13	●	●							
Iowa	●	●	●	●-7	●-13	●	●							●-20
Kansas	●-4	●	●	●-9	●-13	●	●	●	●	●	●		●	●-21
Kentucky	●	●	●	●-7		●	●				●-17			✳
Louisiana	●-3	●-h		●-8	●-14	●	●				●			●
Maine	●	●-h		●-7	●-13	●	●						●	●
Maryland	●-1	●-h	●-6	●-7	●-13	●	●							●-20
Massachusetts	●	●-h		●-7	●-13	●	●							●
Michigan	●	●-2h	●	●-8	●-13	●	●							●-21
Minnesota	●	●		●-7	●-14	●	●							●-21
Mississippi	●			●-8	●-10	●	●				●-17			
Missouri	●	●	●	●-7	●-13	●	●							●
Montana	●-3			●-8		●	●							
Nebraska	●-f			●-7	●-12	●	●							
Nevada	●	●-h	●	●-8	●-13	●	●				●			
New Hampshire	●-3	●-h		●-7	●-13	●	●							●
New Jersey	●-1	●-h	●-6	●-7	●-13	●	●							●
New Mexico	●-1,3	●-h		●-7	●-13	●	●							●-21
New York	●-1	●-h		●-8	●-13	●	●				●-23c			
No. Carolina	●		●	●-7		●	●							
No. Dakota	●-13					●	●							●-21
Ohio	■-3,j	●	●	●-7	●-13	●	●							●-21
Oklahoma	●-3	●-h	●-6	●-8	●-11	●	●				●-17			
Oregon	●-3					●	●							●-21
Pennsylvania	●	●	●-e,#	●-8	●-14	●	●				●-d,#			
Rhode Island	●	●		●-9	●-13	●	●				●-17a			
So. Carolina	●				●-13	●	●							
So. Dakota	●-3	●-h		●-9	●-13	●	●							
Tennessee	●	●-h		●-7	●-13	●	●			●-15			●	
Texas	●				●-13	●	●							
Utah	●-2,3			●-7	●-14	●	●				●-18			
Vermont	●-1	●-h		●-7	●-13	●	●							●
Virginia					86	●	●							
Washington		●-h	●-5	●-8	●-13	●	●						●	●-21
W. Virginia	●-1	●		●-7	●-13	●	●						●	●
Wisconsin	●					●	●				●			●-21
Wyoming	●			●-8	●-13	●	●						●	

● Requirement in law
1 Refactorization
2 Where speeds exceed 35 mph
3 Under 18 years
4 Under 16 years
5 Left side
6 Left and right side
7 One wheel
8 Both wheels
9 Must meet performance standard
10 10" above fasten point
11 12" above fasten point
12 12" above fasten point
13 15" above seat
14 Handgrips below shoulder height
15 Over 750 cc if operator under 18 years

16 Foot wear
17 Speedometer
18 Odometer
19 Annual emissions inspection
20 Random
21 Under 18 years
22 Under 18 years
23 Speedometer with both mile and kilometer calibrations

a If originally equipped by manufacturer
b For motorcycle manufactured after 7/1/74
c For motorcycle manufactured after 9/1/80
d For motorcycle manufactured after 1/1/73
e For motorcycle manufactured after 4/1/77
f Not enforced
g Newer models

h Except if equipped with windscreen
i Except if equipped with windscreen 15" or higher
j Novice license holders
k Manufacturer's requirement for motorcycles manufactured after 1/1/78
m Possession by all; wear under 18 years
Many state inspection regulations require that any equipment installed on a motorcycle must function properly even though the equipment is not required by law.
■ Required by inspection regulations
✳ Denotes removal of requirement since January, 1978 list was distributed.
■ Denotes change in status since January, 1978 list was distributed.

Although this chart represents information from the most authoritative sources available as of the date shown above, the Motorcycle Industry Council is not responsible for accuracy or completeness.

MOTORCYCLE INDUSTRY COUNCIL, INC.

STATE MOTORCYCLE OPERATOR LICENSING PROCEDURES

1979

STATE	Special License or Endorsement	Learner's Permit	Duration of License	Min. Age With Driver Education	Min. Age Without Driver Education	Motorcycle Safety Education a Prereq. to Licensing	Motorcycle Knowledge Test	Off-Road Skill Test	In-Traffic Skill Test	Cycle Inspected	Rider Gear Inspected	Reexamination Required	Reexamined for: Vision	Knowledge	Off-Street	In-Traffic
Alabama	•				14/16[30]											
Alaska	•	•[10]	5		14/16[30]		•		•	•	•	5	•		•[11]	
Arizona	•		3	16	16			•	•		•[34]	3	•	•	•	
Arkansas	•	•[3]	2	14[12]	16	•[13]	•[13]		•	•						
California	•	•[9]	4	16	18		•[15]		•[18]	•		4	•	•		
Colorado	•	•[6]	3	16	16[14]		•[15]			•	•[34]	3	•			
Connecticut	•	⊙[3]	2/4	16	18		•	•	•	•	•[34]					
Delaware	•	⊙[3]	4	16	18		•	•	•	•		4	•			
D.C.	•	⊙[3]	4		16		•	•	•	•		4	•			
Florida	•				15[16]	•[18]	•[15]	•[18]	•[18]	•			•	•		
Georgia	•	•[7]	4	16	16		•[15]			•		4	•	•		
Hawaii	•	⊙[4]	2/4	15	15		•		•	•	•[21]	2/4	•	•		
Idaho				14	16											
Illinois	•	•[9]	3	16[35]	18		•[15]			•	•[34]	9[29]	•			
Indiana				16 yr 1 mo	16 yr 6 mo			•[16]	•[18]			4	•			
Iowa	•		2/4	16	18		•	•	•[18]			2/4	•			
Kansas	•	•[7]	4	16	14[36]		•			•	•		•			
Kentucky	•	⊙[3]	2	16	16			•[18]	•	•						
Louisiana	•		2	15	15		•			•						
Maine	•	⊙[5]	2	16	17	•[32]	•			•						
Maryland	•	⊙[4]	16		16	•	•[15]			•						
Massachusetts	•	⊙[7]	4	16½	17		•	•	•	•		4	•			
Michigan	•	•[6]	4	16	18		•	•[15]	•	•						
Minnesota	•	•[2]	4	16	16	•[22]	•	•	•	•		4	•			
Mississippi				15	15	•[18]	•[18]									
Missouri	•	•[3]	3		16		•	•		•		3	•			
Montana	•	•[7]	4	15	16		•	•			•[20]	4	•			
Nebraska	•	•[9]	4	16	16		•	•		•		4	•	•		•
Nevada	•	•[8]	4		16		•	•		•						
New Hampshire	•	⊙[1]	4		16	•[22]	•	•		•		4	•			
New Jersey	•	⊙[4]	2	17	17		•		•[23]	•		10	•			
New Mexico	•	•[3]	4	15	16	•[24]	•		•[26]	•		2	•			
New York	•	⊙[9]	2/4		16[28]		•	•[19]	•	•		4	•			
North Carolina	•[17]		2/4	18	18		•	•		•		2/4	•			
North Dakota	•	⊙[7]	4	14	16	•[27]	•		•	•						
Ohio	•	⊙[7]	4	16	18		•	•	•	•						
Oklahoma					14[38]	•[25]	•		•[25]	•[25]	•[25]	•[20]				
Oregon			4		16		•	•	•	•	•[20]					
Pennsylvania	•	⊙[5]	2		16		•	•	•	•						
Rhode Island	•	⊙[4]	2	16	18	•[37]	•	•	•	•						
South Carolina	•	•[7]	4	15	15		•	•	•	•		4	•			
South Dakota			4		14		•	•	•	•		4	•			
Tennessee	•		2	16	16[30]		•	•	•	•						
Texas	•	•[9]	4	16	18[33]		•	•	•		•[21]	4	•			
Utah	•	⊙[3]	4	16[31]			•	•	•	•			•	•		
Vermont	•		2	16	18		•	•	•	•						
Virginia	•	•[7]	4	16	18		•	•	•	•		4	•			
Washington	•	•[7]	2	16	16		•	•	•	•						
West Virginia				16	16	•[18]		•[18]								
Wisconsin	•	⊙[7]	2	16	18		•	•		•		3	•	•		•[11]
Wyoming	•	•[9]	3		16		•	•		•						

⊙ Mandatory Learner's Permit Required

1 Maximum 30 days.
2 Maximum 45 days.
3 Maximum 60 days.
4 Maximum 90 days.
5 Maximum 120 days.
6 Maximum 150 days.
7 Maximum 6 months.
8 Maximum 8 months.
9 Maximum 1 year.
10 Maximum 2 years.
11 At the examiner's discretion.
12 Age 14-16, restricted to 250cc or less with parental consent.
13 Age 19 and above, no test with declaration of 1 year of riding experience.
14 Learner's permit issued at age 15½ if enrolled in approved course.
15 Off-street except when facility not available.
16 Age 15, restricted to cycle of 5 brake horsepower-knowledge test only.
17 Required for operating 190cc or larger.
18 "Motorcycle only" license applicants.
19 Provided only at select sites.
20 Only helmet inspected.
21 Helmet inspected for applicants under age 18.
22 Under age 18.
23 14 locations use in-traffic and minimal off-street test.
24 Motorcycle safety education required under age 18 if taught in local school.
25 Required for age 14-15 and "motorcycle only" applicants.
26 Two metro sites conduct off-street tests.
27 Under age 16.
28 Class B (16-18) motorcycle license or permit not valid in New York City; Nassau County has special restrictions.
29 Operators 69 years of age or older required to pass complete examination every 3 years.
30 Age 14-16, restricted to 5 brake horse-power or less.
31 Driver education required regardless of age.
32 Under age 17.
33 Age 15 restricted to 100cc or less.
34 Only eye protection inspected.
35 Age 16-17, restricted to less than 150cc.
36 Age 14-15, restricted license to and from work and school.
37 Required of all first-time applicants regardless of age.
38 Age 14-15, restricted to 125cc or less.

This information was assembled by the Motorcycle Safety Foundation Licensing and Law Enforcement Department. Licensing authorities in all 50 states and the District of Columbia were directly contacted by MSF for an update on the information listed in this chart.

Although this information was obtained from the most authoritative sources available as of December, 1978, the Motorcycle Safety Foundation is not responsible for its accuracy or completeness.

STATE MOTORCYCLE OPERATOR LICENSING — 1979

Beginning in 1974 the Motorcycle Safety Foundation has annually prepared a listing of state procedures for licensing motorcycle operators. This is the third in a series of *Cycle Safety Info* sheets reporting those practices.

As in the past, a detailed questionnaire was sent to the licensing authorities of all 50 states and the District of Columbia. The questionnaire requested information on motorcycle operator license applicant requirements. In 1978 the questionnaire requested additional statistical information about the number of licensed motorcycle and other vehicle operators. That information is included in the table in the adjoining column.

Summary of State Licensing Procedures

- 44 states require a special motorcycle license or endorsement for *all* individuals regardless of age.

- 36 states issue a motorcycle operator learner's permit which allows on-street operation with restrictions.

- 17 states make it mandatory that first-time motorcycle operators obtain a learner's permit before applying for a license.

The time period for the learner's permit ranges from 30 days to two years.

- 25 states allow individuals to get a motorcycle license at an earlier age if they have completed automobile driver education. Minimum ages range from 14 to 17.

- 6 states require motorcycle safety education as a prerequisite to licensing.

- 44 states have a special knowledge test for motorcycle operators.

- 40 states administer some form of an off-road skill test.

- 26 states administer an in-traffic motorcycle operator skill test. 12 of these states routinely give an off-road test in conjunction with the in-traffic test.

- 44 states inspect the motorcycle or check for a valid inspection sticker as part of the licensing process.

- 39 states check to see that the applicant's helmet and eye protection meet state standards.

- 29 states require some form of re-examination. 19 of those states require re-examination every 4 years.

The Motorcycle Safety Foundation is a national, private, nonprofit organization whose goal is the reduction of motorcycle accidents and injuries. This is accomplished through the development and implementation of motorcycle rider education and licensing improvement programs, and through research and public information programs focused on motorcyclist and motorist operations. MSF is sponsored by the five leading motorcycle manufacturers: Honda, Yamaha, Kawasaki, Suzuki and Harley-Davidson.

STATE:	REPORTED MOTORCYCLE LICENSE ENDORSEMENTS	MOTORCYCLE OPERATORS LICENSED IN 1977	TOTAL NUMBER MOTOR VEHICLE OPERATOR LICENSES[1]	TOTAL NUMBER STATE LICENSE EXAMINERS	MOTORCYCLE QUESTIONS INCLUDED ON AUTOMOBILE DRIVER LICENSE KNOWLEDGE TESTS
Alabama	NO MOTORCYCLE TEST		2,500,000	123	NO
Alaska	N/A	N/A	292,000	51	NO
Arizona	N/A	33,690	N/A	68	NO
Arkansas	70,000	N/A	1,500,000	31	NO
California	1,183,949	235,814	19,732,483	480	NO[2]
Colorado	82,296	29,671	2,050,826	150	YES
Connecticut	116,343	N/A	2,070,026	62	NO
Delaware	22,278	3,562	395,000	12	YES
D.C.	N/A	4,600	360,000	12	NO
Florida	NO MOTORCYCLE TEST		6,500,000	474	NO
Georgia	NR	NR	NR	NR	NR
Hawaii	NR	NR	NR	NR	NR
Idaho	NO MOTORCYCLE TEST		N/A	N/A	N/A
Illinois	415,919	N/A	7,000,000	412	YES
Indiana	NO MOTORCYCLE TEST		4,276,266	N/A	YES
Iowa	222,440	N/A	2,085,647	36	YES
Kansas	N/A	N/A	1,777,125	149	NO
Kentucky	N/A	N/A	1,128,917	74	NO
Louisiana	77,635	N/A	2,468,079	260	NO
Maine	46,867	N/A	672,150	33	YES
Maryland	138,921	13,999	2,749,269	105	NO
Massachusetts	N/A	N/A	3,600,000	200	NO
Michigan	416,000	30,110	6,150,000	1,000[4]	YES
Minnesota	172,223	20,612	2,400,000	91	YES
Mississippi	NO MOTORCYCLE TEST		N/A	N/A	N/A
Missouri	NR	NR	NR	NR	NR
Montana	N/A	N/A	556,400	21	NO
Nebraska	61,383	16,770	1,047,893	55	NO
Nevada	N/A	N/A	479,231	35	NO
New Hampshire	62,430	8,763	609,115	27	NO
New Jersey	168,883	N/A	4,951,190	70	NO
New Mexico	NR	NR	NR	NR	NR
New York	295,658	N/A	8,970,091	172	NO
North Carolina	10,185[5]	N/A	3,490,420	257	NO
North Dakota	21,300	2,500	412,000	95	NO
Ohio	430,287	82,146	7,600,000	157	NO
Oklahoma	8,203[3]	N/A	1,872,370	55	N/A
Oregon	160,000	12,100	1,900,000	150	YES
Pennsylvania	363,884	N/A	7,681,883	144	YES
Rhode Island	N/A	N/A	601,248	10	NO
South Carolina	N/A	N/A	1,441,195	97	YES
South Dakota	2,700	564	541,000	27	NO
Tennessee	154,274	N/A	2,611,558	72	YES
Texas	422,708	N/A	8,836,777	343	NO
Utah	128,121	N/A	800,000	55	YES
Vermont	32,113	3,162	325,000	13	NO
Virginia	178,336	61,453	3,287,846	175	NO
Washington	155,791	15,860	2,390,041	191	NO
West Virginia	NO MOTORCYCLE TEST		NR	NR	NR
Wisconsin	184,276	16,773	2,906,580	176	YES
Wyoming	41,444	16,812	314,085	80	NO

N/A — Responded but data not available.

NR — Information not received by print deadline.

NO MOTORCYCLE TEST — State does not have special license for motorcycle operators.

1 Some states reported on other than standard calendar year.
2 Will be included in next revision of automobile test.
3 Motorcycle license required of 14-15 year olds only.
4 All branch office employees authorized to administer skill tests.
5 Motorcycle license law effective 1-1-78.

INDEX